BELLA BATHURST is a writer and [...] include *The Lighthouse Stevenso[...]* Week on BBC Radio 4. Her books [...] for several awards including the 1999 Somerset Maugham Award, the *Guardian* First Book Award, the William Hill Sports Book of the Year and the Crime Writers' Association Gold Dagger. She lives on a farm in Wales.

Praise for *Field Work*

'Highly researched and deeply thoughtful ... Bathurst peers under the bonnet of these lives and reveals things that rarely make it into print. She has a talent for asking the right questions ... *Field Work* is by turns funny, enlightening, frustrating and deeply sad' James Rebanks, *The Times*

'A beautiful hybrid of social history, memoir and nature writing, *Field Work* manages to bring an entire world out of the shadows. [...] Bathurst shows us how interesting all life is if viewed with the correct mixture of sympathy and curiosity' Alex Preston, *Observer*

'A priceless portrait of one of the least understood and frequently most vilified of people: farmers. It should really be read by all in this country who buys food – i.e. everyone. If anyone wants to understand farming better, I would press this book into their hands ... The writing is at once tough and lyrical, unsentimental, piercingly truthful and observant ... heart-wrenching as well as dryly funny ... *Field Work* is a superb testament to that way of life, and richly demonstrates what a terrible loss that would be – for all of us' Book of the Week, *Daily Mail*

'A vivid portrait of a fast-changing world' *Telegraph Summer Reads*

FIELD WORK

FIELD WORK

What Land Does to People and
What People Do to Land

BELLA BATHURST

P

PROFILE BOOKS

This paperback edition first published in 2022

First published in Great Britain in 2021 by
Profile Books Ltd
29 Cloth Fair
London
ECIA 7JQ
www.profilebooks.com

Copyright © Bella Bathurst, 2021, 2022

3 5 7 9 10 8 6 4 2

Typeset in Sabon by MacGuru Ltd
Printed and bound by CPI Group (UK) Ltd, Croydon CR0 4YY

The moral right of the author has been asserted.

A CIP catalogue record for this book is available
from the British Library.

ISBN 978 1 78816 214 2
eISBN 978 1 78283 531 8

Contents

While the earth remaineth, seedtime and harvest, and cold and heat, and summer and winter, and day and night shall not cease.

King James Bible, Genesis 8:22

Introduction

The first time I saw Bert he was walking up the lane back to the farm. His head was bent and his shoulders were round and a rough foam of hair had blown loose round the back of his collar. He was wearing wellies and an old Barbour, its pockets sagged and one of its shoulders come away at the seams. His centre of gravity was low to the ground and he walked with a steady concentrated roll, swaying solidly up the lane like a boat at a mooring. When he heard the sound of my car he altered course until he was on a diagonal trajectory to the verge. He looked up as I passed, a clear assessing squint: good or bad, friend or foe. There was something in his presence which reminded me of a badger: grounded, stubborn, utterly British.

I was coming to see about renting the farm cottage, so it was his wife Alison whom I met first. We sat in the kitchen with biscuits between us talking about roadworks. The cottage had only just gone up on Rightmove, but they'd already had eight different applicants come to view: people with dogs, people who couldn't drive, people with two-hour commutes. The dogs were a deal-breaker for a start, she said. It didn't matter how well-trained the owners claimed they were (and owners always said their dogs were practically vegan): the Howells had lost stock before. An Alsatian staying in one of the holiday cottages over the hill had once got loose in the field and ripped the throat out of two ewes. The couple had paid up without protest and flitted the following night, but no one was going to take the chance again. Between the chatter Alison was making it clear that we were engaged in an interview for the position of tenant, and that the story was a test. Whose side would I take – owner, farmer, or dog?

Bert arrived half an hour later, taking his accustomed place in the armchair by the table. There followed some hard questions (what kind of gardener was I? Had I experience of living on a farm? What did I know about sheep?) followed by more overt bargaining: rent, deposit, furnishings. I left knowing both that I had liked them and that they had liked me. Sure enough, a day later Alison rang me and said if I wanted it, I'd got the tenancy.

Rise Farm is a 180-acre hill farm in Wales. From the valley below the land lifts upwards so gently that you barely notice the climb until the view turns and you find yourself looking down on a river several hundred feet below. These are the foothills of the Black Mountains, and this is the crossing point for two different weather systems: sun in the east, rain in the west. The land is south-facing and fertile, but at 800 metres above sea level it's too steep for growing arable crops.

The farm has been in Bert's family for four generations, providing a rough but steady living for over a century. Bert's dad Gerwyn took over the farm from his father in the 1930s. Bert was the only boy out of five children and, though his sisters were as essential to the running of the farm as he was, no one ever doubted who would succeed. At the village school his teachers always understood that Edward the Confessor and the Past Imperfect were locked in a losing fight with silaging for the attention of their students. At harvest time half the school would vanish into the fields and, during lambing, most would turn up an hour or so late in the morning owlish from lack of sleep.

By 2013 Bert and Alison were farming 300 sheep, participating in the Rural Stewardship Scheme and taking the Single

Farm Payment. Except for occasional help from visiting vet students, they dealt with everything themselves. David, their son, was in Spain, and their daughter Sarah had recently married and moved over to Somerset. That year the Howells' income was £72,000 and their outgoings were £76,000. They had the rent from the only farm cottage and had recently allocated a couple of fields on which to grow three hay crops a year for a neighbour's anaerobic digester.

Once I moved, things settled into a rhythm. A couple of times a week Bert would come down the lane on the quad, hunched over the handlebars like a cyclist taking a tricky finish. At that stage they had two dogs, Bryn and a collie who for a year or so I genuinely believed to be called Come Here You Useless Bugger. Whatever the weather and however apparently informal, Bert's weekly check-ups always had an air of the state visit about them. Back in the 1970s he had done most of the building work to the house, walling, insulating and extending what had originally been a two-room labourer's cottage, slating the roof and adding a proper kitchen. Knowing every stone of it, he now took more than a merely financial interest in its welfare. He would open the gate and walk along the path with his hands clasped behind his back, stopping every few yards to note the position of the wheelie bins and checking the fritillaries for insubordination. Though his visits were regular he'd always arrive with a pretext: he'd come to enquire about the cistern, he'd come to look at the guttering, he'd come to consider the electrics in the shed.

'Hello, stranger!' he'd say, leaning one hand against the wall to pull his boots off. 'Where was you this time?' Or, in summer, nodding at the lawn, 'What I going to say, you could do with a mower on that.'

There was an etiquette to this. He never stayed longer than an hour, never took more than one cup of tea, always sat in

3

the same chair. Outside the buzzards mewed and the planes passed over while the dogs made their own tour of inspection, glaring at the chickens and peeing importantly on the septic tank. When I showed him something I'd made – a table, a box – he would turn it over, running his thumb along the grain. If he didn't like it he'd ask what it was for. If he did, he'd say nothing at all.

He'd tell me stories about the farm or the news from that week's market. Back in the early twentieth century the Howells were tenants on the land, paying an annual rent of £143. When Rise Farm was put up for sale in 1920 Bert's granddad had taken out a mortgage and bought the place. The price had included a well-founded stone farmhouse, stabling for five horses, a chaff house, 'a cowshed for six with range and calves' cot, two barns, an engine house, two granaries, sheds for the wagons and carts, water from a spring, and 180 acres of land'.

There had been a farm here for a very long time. Nobody really knew how old this place was, but there was good evidence that parts of it dated back to the fifteenth century. Like many farms it had started out small, but over the years it had wandered off westwards and was by now so often overwritten it had become an impacted scribble of alleyways, improvised partitions and odd-shaped sheds. In the milking parlour there was a staircase which went nowhere except the ceiling. The old piggery had become a parking area, and the granary where for decades the old horse had walked in circles round the millwheel was now a storage shed. As on many farms, the rise and fall and rise of its fortunes was inscribed in each succeeding building material: stone, brick, oak, concrete, breeze-block, steel, asbestos, glass, UPVC, solar panels, tin.

This area has always been mostly agricultural – no coal and not much industry – which meant that anyone who couldn't work on their family farms got out, seeding themselves all over the world: London, Canada, Idaho, New Zealand, Argentina, Newfoundland. Those who remained made the best of what the land gave them, including the materials. Outbuildings on many farms round here have so often been altered and rebuilt that they have taken on the asymmetry of man-made geology: the waney seam of a long-gone chimney breast, the wrinkles of a vast oak lintel slumped beneath the weight of its years. Bits of old sheds have been buttressed with scaffolding and others with stone, arrow-slit vents bricked up then unpicked, rafters now jowled with cobwebs and haynets, retaining walls drifting towards the brooks or subsiding into the hill. Over the centuries a line that once seemed rock solid might gradually find its rationality meandering off into something a little more natural. Everything got used and reused; buildings rose and fell, recycled infinitely from the same stone and slate, patched in, hand-set, chipped, dressed and redressed, everything staying exactly the same but changing all the time. Every few decades the farm would expand or inhale according to the particular winds of change: a war, a recession, a shift in political direction.

During the First World War the government requisitioned all wheat and hay stocks to feed men and horses at the Front, paying a standard £20 per ton. When the money stopped in 1920, the whole country suffered. In 1939 the local War Ag Committee had required the Howells to turn their land over to potatoes and sugar beet, though by 1950 the farm had reverted to its old mixture: around 220 ewes and lambs, 12 pigs, 50 chickens and 18 cattle, 5 of whom provided milk for the family and beyond. Around 18 acres of the flattest land was planted with mixed corn and barley, half an acre was still down to potatoes and 9 were growing mangolds or swedes for use as winter fodder. Until Bert's granddad had bought the first tractor in the

1940s, all carting, hauling, harrowing, ploughing and harvesting was done by the two horses, Betsy and Prince. They could be temperamental – Prince had a habit of wandering off if left too long in the shafts – but they were often better-natured than the machinery which could roll out of control on the high banks down near the brook. As in many steeper areas of the country, horses continued to be used around here until well into the 1960s.

Then as now the land was always considered to be best suited to sheep. Shearing was done by hand and the fleeces were sold on to local spinners. Tails were docked at six weeks, and a ferocious mixture of Stockholm Tar, sheep dip and Mintic powder was used to kill or cure most ills. TB testing for the cattle was made compulsory in the 1960s, and Bert and his sisters grew quick and clever at milking before school every morning. Until recently, 180 acres had been a respectable size for a farm, allowing not only self-sufficiency for the household but also an adaptable surplus which could be turned from sheep to beet to cows to wheat. Everything that the land offered was used: pigeons, rabbits, damsons, sloes, apples, bracken. The stones cleared from the fields became the walls around those fields, the trees felled by gales were raised to second lives as gate posts or purlins.

This place, this land, wasn't a job or a business: it was everything – past and future, identity and rhythm, daily bread and Sunday rest. But places like these were struggling now. Too small for the future and too poor in the past, their version of agriculture seemed good for nothing except a museum. Now, the drive was all for volume or intensity: a few crops on a lot of land, or lots of crops in a digital field. The margins were too small for places like this. The market for lamb was declining and upland like this wasn't worth the inputs. Best thing for it was to rewild or try glamping.

Sometimes I'd meet Bert out in the lane, and once he'd brought me up to date on any recent news he'd stand for a second looking out. Below us the land stretched out, terraced by hedgerows and velveted with distant woodland. The ravens clanked.

'See there?' Bert indicated a flattish field on the flank of the opposite ridge. 'Long Field – see where he's bare in the right corner?'

I look over at a green rectangle half a mile away, edged off with quickthorn but to my eyes just like all its neighbours.

'There. Si Davis's field. In't ever been right. Don't matter what Si does, he's always bald in that part. Been years when it been drought and when the grass goes dry you see there's something there.'

Like what?

'This whole part, this was fighting ground. There's things beneath – forts, castles.'

So there's a ruin under there. And there – he pointed again over the western edge of the bank. Back in the 1950s that small steep patch was the subject of a forty-year dispute between brother and sister, which ended in both their downfalls. Now half the bank belonged to a big local farmer (1,800 sheep, 150 beef sucklers) who, when he had found his nice clean Beltexes infected with scab by his neighbour's flock, had sent one of the neighbour's ewes down the bank to him with the letters **F U** sheared neatly into its fleece.

Bert points out a faint line, almost erased, crossing the field below the farmhouse from west to east. It was once a path which led eastwards towards the English border. During the agricultural depression of the 1920s unemployment had forced many farm labourers to walk down off the hills to the poor-house in the next village. Old maps still showed the path, though it had fallen under the plough again during the Second

World War. Someone from the local parish council had recently come to talk to Bert about reopening it as a public path. The meeting had been brief but clear. 'Never heard anything so stupid in all my days. I told him to get from here and don't come back, look.'

And there, over near the little copse on the eastern side. On the reverse of the hill there's a patch of steep wood which had once been the site of the Great Vanishing Horse Scandal. At some point in the 1770s, horses started disappearing from fields and stables all over the county. At that time a good farm horse would have had the same value as a good farm tractor now, but, no matter what protections owners put in place, the thefts continued. For a long time no one could find any trace of the missing horses, and it was only years later when a chance tip-off led owners to a small wood on a hill that the solution was discovered: a disused iron-ore mine well curtained with ivy where, down the old tunnels and into the hill, a complete underground network of stables had been constructed. One of the local farmers had been taking the horses, keeping them for a while, altering their appearance and then selling them on.

Bert would point out the house half a mile off and tell me every dip and spike of that family's fortunes over the past five decades – the depressive father, the barrister daughter, the half-million they'd borrowed for goats, the peculiar venture into pasturage or IT. Or he'd talk about the field beside us: how the grass was behaving in this first week of March compared to last year, what it meant pound for pound to the sheep, whether they'd be able to get anything out of the low field after a week of frosts or a month of fogs. He knew it because he'd walked it, ploughed it and watched a thousand days of rain chase over it. He'd cut its thistles, lifted its stones, trimmed its footings, and seen droughts lay bare its bones. He'd dug the drains for it, provided a water supply, made sure there was shade in summer

8

or cover in winter. He knew the weeks when the grass did best for cattle (longer strands that they could get their tongues around), and when it best fattened sheep (shorter grass, better for ripping). He knew the birds which nested in the same places year after year, the spot where the deer always got in, the butterflies that had come and the moths which had gone. He knew the years when rabbits or crows had picked off half the crop, the seasons which had come good and the years gone wrong. He knew the burr in the ash by the hedge that the tups liked to scratch and the hidden places without reeds where the water still sprang. He knew where the earth was at its best and the patch where only docks would grow. He knew which week the blackthorn whitened at the base of the hill and the knuckle of concrete where the trailer always tripped. He knew the high-tide mark for the brook in flood and the years when it had overtopped it. He knew the middens, tips and dumps where the old shed asbestos was buried and exactly what had happened to the missing batch of Cymag and dynamite. He knew how this earth behaved in every season, and he talked about the taste and sweetness of the grass as though he drank it. Too much rain and the grass would be thin and empty, washed of nourishment. Too little, and it would be low and sour. When the fields flooded the ewes' feet would rot and the water would drip into their wool, acting on them as it would on a human standing in a downpour in three wet jerseys. Too cold, and the new lambs might perish. Too hot, and they could dehydrate. If the sheep didn't put on weight then they had to be brought in and fattened up on the hay cut last summer. If they still didn't put on weight then they wouldn't fetch a decent price when sold, but if they were overweight they weren't worth what had been spent on them.

Bert also knew the ewes who would make good mothers and the feckless types who would shrug off their own lambs. He knew the tricks to lure one ewe into taking another mother's orphans and the patience required to sit up all night alone in a frozen shed with a pen full of complications. He watched the thieves – the ewes who would steal another lamb to practise on and then reject their newly stolen goods once they'd had their own, the dominant characters and the quiet ones. He'd been pulling lambs out of ewes every spring for sixty years, and he knew all there was to know about birth, death and all the money in between. He'd never been to London or Swansea. He'd been to Cardiff once for the rugby, but he didn't miss it. He thought nothing of his own knowledge. The world didn't rate his skills, so how should he?

In the public mind, farming had become like the police. Once the sort of profession which the middle classes respected without really understanding, now it had become the sort of profession which everyone disrespected without really understanding either. Now if you told someone you were a farmer they'd come back at you with something about chemicals or welfare. Farmers were murderers. Or poisoners. Or soil-plundering asset-strippers. Or they were benefit cheats, tax-dodgers, system-milking criminals. Farmers never stopped complaining. It was never right. Always it seemed to be too wet, too dry, too cold, too hot, too windy, too soft, too hard. There they were, on the radio or the TV, wanting something, having a go. No one seemed to pinpoint exactly what farmers had done that was so bad, but everyone knew they had. They were taking the taxpayer for a ride. They were ripping us off, pilfering the best of our good nature. And no one understood the time it took, the hope it used up, the unrelenting gamble in pulling a life out of earth.

Everyone who saw the view from Rise Farm marvelled at its perfect representation of perfect British countryside, at the absence of car noise and the presence of so many birds. Over in one corner electricity pylons strode across the land, in another there was the low green roof line of a new chicken shed. In winter, car headlights plunged out of the lanes like the lights of divers, brightness flaring for a second against the unpolluted dark.

But it didn't take long to realise that everyone also saw that same view in their own way. Blow-ins like me saw this place lengthwise – a great wide spread of fields and hedges, a well-worked sliver of Britain. We took in the view and saw everything together all the way from the hill to the river, a single indiscriminate image of stability. One field was like the next field, one wood looked much the same as another, and this view was probably just a comparison to a different countryside somewhere else. Here in this part of Wales there were hedges, but if you drove north, the fields would be divided by walls. Here the old buildings were stone, but 50 miles to the east, they would be brick. Here there were hills, but if you went west there would be mountains. All the people who came to Rise from elsewhere saw it in relation to London or Manchester, a soft dull opposite to the hard, exciting lines of a city. This was the Britain you would see if you flew above – a reworked land, every liveable stitch of it pulled and sworn and worked and worked again until in some places the colour had all rubbed off and all you could see was just a dunnish smudge of human energy.

Agricultural bureaucrats looked at that view and saw a classification. According to the EU and DEFRA (the Department for Environment, Food and Rural Affairs, the government department responsible for agriculture in the UK), Rise was an upland grazing livestock farm on a Less Favoured Area. This itself was a classification further split into Disadvantaged and Severely Disadvantaged, and was considered to encompass areas of rough hillside, heath and semi-improved grassland. Sometimes Less Favoured Areas were themselves also in Areas Facing Natural Constraints or participants in a Higher-Level Rural Stewardship Scheme. They could also be holdings on Sites of Special Scientific Interest or in National Parks, Areas of Outstanding Natural Beauty, Special Protection Areas, Ramsar Wetlands or any one of several other acronyms denoting 'significant agricultural, landscape, archaeological, recreational, cultural and natural resource value', and thus subject to their own turbulent regulatory microclimates. Maps showed the curves of the land flattened into acronyms (NIAs including Near-Miss NIAs, NNRs, SSSIs, SPAs, SACs, PHIs, WFDMCs), the blur of reality coded into manageable departments.

Campaigners saw this as a desolation. Yes, there were trees, but the ash was living on borrowed time, the oak was under threat and every living thing was flayed by grazing at one end and felling at the other. True, there were hedges, but they were always razored down to a clinical finish, giving the fledglings no time to fly. Above us there were cameras, below us there were poisons and what looked like good wild health was just a last gasp. The fields were full of white ovine maggots, the songbirds were killed by cars and cats, there was slurry in the rivers and when it rained the soil bounded in fat red rivers down the roads and out of the county. Energy crops like maize were raping the earth's fertility, the grasslands were down to no more than three species and the cows were just high-yield genetic slaves. This place was an unhappy illusion, a mere green death mask.

Lettings agents saw this place as a commodity – 25 per cent extra on a weekend rental for the privilege of a piece of green like that. Convert the mill, add an en-suite to the cart shed, and you could work that strip of sky until it made more than the animals you had on it. In many areas of Britain the more beautiful the land, the harder it is to farm. The Yorkshire

Dales, the Lake District, the Scottish Highlands, Snowdonia – all ravishing, all for sale at roughly half the price per acre of prime arable land. It's not an equation which always works: most of Cornwall, the Cotswolds and Perthshire manage both looks and money – but anyone coming for a weekend break wants to see something which conforms to their notion of what this country is: green, more green, maybe some hills, a beach. A sliver of river can double the value of a property, a harbour increase it by more than 80 per cent. If anything, the actual farming was a disadvantage: smelly, noisy, and incompatible with quiet rural lie-ins.

And all of us had an opinion, and all expected to be listened to. We all ate food and lived in some sort of an environment, whether it was urban or challenging or oxygen-deprived, so therefore we all had an opinion on the countryside. We wanted it to look and sound a certain way, conform to certain laws, remain worked but not working. Our demands from the land increased while the number of people who tended it decreased. Farmers now suddenly found themselves summoned by Whats-App to the village hall to account for their use of glyphosates or be taken to task on their hedge-trimming schedule.

But that same countryside looked very different when you saw it as a business. Both the farmhouse and the farm cottage at Rise have no south-facing windows. No windows, in other words, to face the thing outsiders most savour. 'That was work,' Bert said. 'Why'd you want to come in the house at night and be looking at what you been doing all day?'

When he was describing it, the detail Bert could pull out of a single sliver of field was as rich as lace. But his precision was mostly invisible. If the bureaucrats and the incomers saw this place horizontally then Bert saw it vertically. Down through the soil and deep through the generations. He saw the boundaries between his land and the next with the same us-and-them finality a Londoner might see the hidden borders of gang territories. This field here, this tree, this beast, was as intimate to him as family, but that field there belonging to his neighbour, that was foreign land, as far from him as the Arctic. This was home, that was away. The fields in the distance had their own history and traditions. The individuals around them belonged to that land just as Bert belonged to this, and it was more than a life's full work to learn one farm completely. For him, Rise wasn't an income or a classification or a family or a business or a job. It was everything.

And yet each of us – the farmer, the bureaucrat, the tourist, the campaigner, the tenant, the estate agent, the agronomist – saw the same physical facts cropped to fit our own focus. All of us saw it through our own frames of purpose or imagination, and all of us required this land to be a part of what it was not. Maybe it was a dreary rustic cliché full of old white folk and boring walks. Or it was outstanding raptor habitat – prime nesting sites, good small mammal predation prospects. Maybe it was the potential of next year's harvest or the challenge of better grass. Maybe it was the future, a proof of a life meaningfully spent and a future well prepared. All of us wanted something from it, even if that thing was only a dream. None of us would ever just let it be.

I'm not a farmer, and I didn't grow up on a farm. I'm an Anglo-Scot, the product of a father from Gloucestershire and a mother from Lanarkshire, and I've spent much of my life flitting between city and countryside, going from the centre of nowhere to the middle of everything. I spent twenty years living and working in London and Scotland, playing games with the seasons, accelerating or reversing, spinning back two weeks or leaping forwards by four. In the journeys up and down between

the two countries I could watch the year turn from daffodil
north to rosy south in the space of a few hours, while the ther-
mometer might shift by ten degrees or more.

But when I got to Rise Farm the leaps got less abrupt. The
more time I spent there or with farming neighbours the more
I understood I didn't understand. What I thought I knew of
farming was based on living beside it, not within it. Every year
as children we'd gone to the local agricultural show, hauled
the family dog (bribed, not heavily enough) round the show
ring and admired the Champion Leek (4-foot, inedible). With
a smirk of mockery we'd passed the boys clustered around the
Massey Ferguson stand and, aged a foot-and-a-half, had stood
awestruck at approximately testicle height by the Charolais
bull pens. We got our eggs from the back seat of the neighbour's dead Datsun and our cream by swinging a big plastic
bucket into a multi-gallon tank in which the just-milked milk
slopped silkily through the tanker pipes. There was a tran-
quillity in watching the rich white liquid lick the steel walls,
drawling against the swirl of the blades. But none of that was
farming. That was just watching farming.

I'd spent years in places surrounded by sheep or cattle who
came and went according to some remote generational logic I
didn't really follow. Fields of wheat or barley came and went,
turned from brown to green to gold, were formed into round
or square bales, became black plastic. The tractors in them
moved slowly up and down brown plough lines through wheeling crowns of crows and gulls. There was mud on the road or
there wasn't, there was a herd of cows in the lane or not. The
ewes in the next field could be small and fine-faced or square
and thuggish. Sometimes there were no sheep at all. The buildings looked stoic: slits for windows, slats for walls. The fields
were fallow or overworked, poxed with molehills or bald from
overgrazing. They contained experiments – biomass trees,

dog agility courses, wind turbines – or scrambler tracks and
gravel quarries. The lower ones were a fixedly unreal green, the
upper ones patched with heather or bracken. Grass grew, sped
upwards, swayed to the swell of the wind, was cut, grew, swelled
again. Winter came, the animals vanished, spring came, the
animals reappeared and all the time the laws of the farming calendar appeared only as moving shadows flitting against other
dramas. The byres and steadings kept their backs to the road,
and what went on inside those places was just somebody else's
story. Everyone shared certain things – the snow, the length of
winter, bad broadband, road closures – but always there stayed
the same separation between species.

I began to understand things differently once I got to
Rise. Farming, it seemed, embodied so many switchbacks. It
was seen as insular, but required to be global. It had a reputation for being secretive, yet you could see it from space. It
required everlasting reserves of emotional resilience from
a group of people who never talked. It was seen as lazy and
low-status, but I'd never come across a group of people who
worked harder. It was seen as ossified, but most farmers were
meant to be eight professions in one day, from accountant to
vet, mechanic to economist, midwife to chemist, manager to
gambler. A gambler most of all. Its workforce was tiny and
declining, but it had more hold over Britain's sense of self than
anything except perhaps the sea and the Beatles. Shakespearean
family dramas unravelled over generations in places that only
inspectors and vets ever went to. It lived by a set of different
regulations, had separate lawyers and accountants, needed a
separate government department, abided by footnotes, exemptions, addendums. It had done more to influence our history
than half our wars. It seemed to be the exception to every rule,
but it still provided the basics of existence. What it did could
lurch in the space of days from rustic irrelevance to first on the

agenda. I couldn't see how a bunch of people who spent their whole lives dealing with sex, death and paperwork, or who at the very least spent a lot of time producing our food, could be considered separate, or lazy. Or, for that matter, low-status.

And it seemed to have moved so far, so fast. In the space of a generation it had gone from being a well-regarded profession stood solidly at the centre of British life to something regarded as semi-criminal. Everywhere you looked it seemed as though farmers were either vast grasping grain barons driving 90-metre combines and skiing all over the subsidy, or were held up with habit and baler twine living in conditions disdained by goats. But the farmers I came across were as varied and various as the land they farmed. Some farmed thousands of acres and millions in credit. Some had no debt, but no food either. Some looked after pigs or sheep, and some strawberries or firewood. Some said they'd discourage their children from coming into the business; others relied on it. Some said you did have to be born to it, and some said you didn't. Some said it was a vocation, some said there was nothing that separated it from any other business. Farmers were as infinite in age, condition and outlook as mothers are.

There were a few things that they did have in common. Almost everyone in farming works hard. Everyone hates uncertainty but is used to it. And, though it is changing, at the moment almost everyone is white, old and male. There was one final similarity. All the farmers I spoke to were refreshingly, endearingly honest. All of them told truth. Not *the* Truth – whatever that might be – but the truth as they saw it. It might not have been a truth others liked or agreed with, but there was very little question as to the honesty of the person who spoke it, whoever they were and whatever the ground they stood on.

Often I was met with a kind of defiant, arms-folded pride: *here you go this is how it is challenge me I dare you.* I also kept coming across tight professional groups who are all skilled at and proud of what they do but who have often found themselves at the wrong end of public opinion. They may be fulfilled in their jobs, but they are also braced for trouble. Most of the time I understood that any animosity wasn't directed at me but at what – or who – might stand behind my digital recorder. Sometimes in their responses I heard the voices they'd had to answer in the past – animal welfare campaigners, inspectors suspicious of their habits, people who expected them to be unfeeling killers in a fallen world. Or maybe just small lamb-loving children asking hard questions. Covid-19 and lockdown gave them both a new set of troubles and a new lease of life: suddenly everyone was discussing flour again.

Once they had decided to let me in, almost everyone was overwhelmingly generous with their time and what they revealed. They talked with intensity and humour about their understanding of the world and what this earth meant to them. All of those individuals placed their trust in me, and I've tried to uphold that. In many cases, I've anonymised the people and the places in this book, and in some cases I've changed identifying details. But what they said and what I saw remains just as it was.

The only variation to that openness were the larger holdings with big-name clients selling our standard kitchen essentials – eggs, chickens, chips, burgers. The clients all employed sizeable Comms Teams, reinforcing walls of PRs and Relationship Managers who wore polo shirts and reflective wraparound shades and didn't return repeated requests for interviews. The Teams talked with trained sunniness about inspiring forward-thinking innovation and harvesting sustainable resources and acting as environmental beacons and provided long shining waterfalls of data to support their arguments. They saw the future of farming as big: big acreages, big numbers, big money, big yields. They all had unbelievable smiles. At Open Farm Sundays they brought interpretation boards and haybales and let the kids turn the steering wheels of the big yellow tractors. There were artisanal product tasters and face painting and everyone did their best to look friendly while actually being as friendly as a slammed door. Though each farm was often on contract to several clients (say, two supermarkets and one fast-food producer), each of those client's Teams talked of the place as 'our farm' and 'our farmers'. Strangely, many of 'their farmers' were nowhere to be seen.

Though plenty of the McBucket Special Forces came from farming backgrounds themselves, they regarded the old 100-acre holdings, the Rise Farm types, as nostalgic and indulgent. If the British public continued to insist on cheap food then the only realistic future was to make farms larger – amalgamate, swallow the little places, beef up the economies of scale, double-muscle every farm. Everyone liked a good view, but the countryside – all of it, everywhere – had to pay its way. We had a choice. Either we could accept a landscape which included polytunnels and solar farms, or we could shut up and get our chicken chlorinated from Kansas. The irony was, they may well have been right. They certainly had compelling points to make about how we eat and at what cost. But the language they used always seemed to slide off the page. Under the unsleeping gaze of their CCTV, 'their farmers' sometimes had the look of people who had themselves been milked.

It was hard too to find accounts to trust. There were plenty of books, papers and articles about farming: conventional vs organic, livestock vs arable. Often they were polemical: we should be eating less meat, we should be rewilding, we should be reintroducing more native breeds, making meadows, protecting pollinators. Or they were guided by the fashions of farming policy: farms must increase yield, decrease nitrates, have better welfare standards. But whichever direction they were coming from, all of them were talking about farming, not farmers.

I was curious to know what made this profession so different. The longer I spent at Rise the more I looked for something that told me about the individuals, not the systems. I wanted to know about the psychology of this life and the grain of that bond between man and land. The best I could do would be to stand and translate – to see that same view down the hill the way Bert saw it, but also the way someone from a city might. Perhaps inevitably, the result is skewed towards the west and Wales – Powys, Shropshire, Warwickshire, Herefordshire, Carmarthen. In part, that's because it's the area closest to where I live. But it's also an agricultural area with a wide variety of different farm types, from huge soft-fruit businesses to tiny upland sheep farms. This is my attempt to understand a little bit of what people do to land, and what land does to people.

1

Fallen Stock

It starts with an end.

One bright morning in the middle of May, Ian Carswell comes sliding to a halt in a Tenbury car park. I'm perched by the floral arrangement and he's in a tipper lorry. It's a smallish thing with raw grey sides and nothing distinctive about it, the sort of truck which carries topsoil or aggregate all over the country. The only thing which might give a clue to its true purpose is the small blue 'Andersons' lettering on both doors.

'Jump in,' says Ian, leaning over and prodding open the passenger door.

The cab smells of self-consciousness and lemon air-freshener. Ian wouldn't normally allow a passenger, and almost certainly wouldn't be taking one now if the boss hadn't told him to. This is his space and his long-standing office, the place where he has spent the best part of his life, more personal to him than home. Over the years he has customised everything here to suit his purposes, and everything now shows the marks of unflinching use. The dials on the air-con have faded and a couple of the steering-wheel levers are supported with a light tracery of duct tape while the space between the seats contains a customised filing system, including a box of fresh job sheets and forms, several pens and a slot for completed paperwork.

On the dashboard are a phone and transmitter, and above the windscreen there's a tracker and satnav. Once in a while the tracker beeps, but Ian never even switches on the GPS. Over the course of a working day, he may travel between 100 and 300 miles, but he's been driving this area for so long he knows every road, lane, track and shortcut within a hundred-mile radius of Shropshire better than most London cab drivers know King's Cross to Blackfriars. Behind the driver's seat are the tools of Ian's trade: a captive bolt gun, a set of blanks and a blue plastic pithing rod.

He has, he says, already worked out most of today's route. Barring any unexpected changes of plan we're starting in Tenbury, going east towards Bridgnorth, covering the fringes of Kidderminster, then round into Wales and back down again via Ludlow. Several call-outs came in yesterday, the office has already been on to him about several more, and he's expecting a run of new instructions this morning as clients catch up after the bank holiday. He'll have to patch each one into his route as they come in, endlessly recalibrating his own internal map to take account of the size, urgency and distance of each job. Andersons has eight drivers collectively covering the West Midlands from a base just over the Welsh border. Every day, each one loops out from the centre in a ragged oval, stopping, picking up, moving on. If their working journeys were traced on a map, the resulting image would look something like the petals of a flower, each route blooming out from Bewdley or Newtown or Cleehill until collectively they capillarise much of Wales and Western England.

Beyond the windows the country rushes past in an endless pattern-repeat: field, wood, dealership, fencing, farm, pub, garage, rail bridge, road sign, big house, small house. The cab is high enough to peer over the hedges at the swell of greening grass: two agricultural feed suppliers, a stately home exposed in its empty parkland, hay bales in fodder bins ringed in brown hoof-prints like crop circles, wires, pylons. A month ago this landscape was down to the bone: dun-brown with fatigue, the silvery clavicles of old roots poking through the topsoil, snowdrops flattened under fresh tyre tracks. Now everything is softened and made hopeful by spring, the threat of winter receding into the earth again. On a morning like this everything in these fields looks eternal, a day that has nothing to do with death.

Ian, meanwhile, is concentrating on his schedule, sitting with the steering wheel held in front of him like a man before a Sunday roast. He's big, but the bulk is mainly muscle, and he's both fit and agile. Round-faced, strong-shouldered, a balding man with a dark moustache. He wears a small pair of thin-rimmed glasses, a blue work shirt with 'MT Andersons' across the top-left pocket, a pair of black wellies, a digital watch (consulted frequently) and the remote control for the tipper winch slung round his neck.

Ian is a driver with forty-five years' experience working for a large fallen-stock operator nearby. Or rather, Ian is a knacker-man, knackering being the old name for a role which over the past fifty years has been entirely modernised. His job and the way he conducts it are unrecognisable from the profession he originally came into. Now, there's forms, procedures, trucks, lifters, legislation. Testing for BSE is mandatory on any animal over forty-eight months, and any new drivers coming to the role have to be fully licensed and certified. A business which was once a byword for the wrecked and smelly ends of animal life is now as antiseptic as modern biosecurity regulations can make it.

But in the essentials, knackering is as it always was. Ian and his colleagues deal with the animals which for one reason or another do not thrive: the sick or lame or old, the ones which never got close to being old, the cows condemned, the pigs with broken legs, the orphan lambs which took one look at life and quit, the horses on their last legs, the sickly ewes and surplus bull calves. These are the animals who will never leave home or face the long final journey to the nearest abattoir. In their case, the executioner comes to them.

Like farming itself, knackering is governed by the seasons. Despite all of agriculture's efforts to even out seasonal peaks and troughs there are still more deaths in winter and spring. Even with stock indoors, cold and infection still kill off the weak or the soft. Spring brings the diseases of growth: too much too quickly, or not enough for too long. Summer could mean either drought or rain, and then it's back into autumn – early frosts, gales and hail. And then, year-round, there are the plagues of economics: animals which may well be healthy but which could only be raised at a loss.

In this case it's the Tuesday after a bank holiday weekend, three days strafed with thunderstorms, sudden downpours and shifts in temperature so sharp the roads smoke. Animals don't like these leaps and plunges any more than humans do. Young lambs may not be able to tolerate the lurch from warm day to evening chill, and these murky, fevered days of summer breed fly-strikes – flies laying their eggs in the sheep's fleece, producing maggots which then feed off wounds which can prove fatal if left unchecked. And that's without the year-round hazards of cast sheep (pregnant ewes who have rolled over and can't get up again), cows with mastitis, sheep with scrapie or scab or liver fluke. The deaths go on all the time, quietly, unobserved, in the corners of fields and byres, warmed or unwarmed by the sun. Thunderstorms are a different matter. Lightning goes to ground down the closest tall object. If that happens to be a tree, the roots and ground will take up the charge and lead it through to whatever – or whoever – is sheltering beneath, meaning that several animals can be killed or hurt at once.

Half the skill of his job, Ian points out, is the tracking. If the forecast says there's going to be storms then he can most likely predict an increase in call-outs, but if, after two weeks of bad weather, it's going to be sunny and windless then farmers might finally have a chance to find the hill ewe who slipped down a gully, or the horse who chose a fine spring morning to jump too far. Likewise, it's the daily mental route-mapping and the joining-up of one job (dead cow, tricky access) with another (live boar, no further information) into a seamless and economical day's driving. There's also the matter of how best to load. The tipper takes up to a certain weight, and once that weight is reached Ian has to return to HQ, unload, disinfect and then head out again. Driving all the way back to the depot in the middle of the day takes time – time that would be better spent on the road – so if at all possible he wants to load in such a way that he's doing the lighter animals (sheep) at the beginning and the heavier ones (cows) at the end.

Even so, he's got fifteen jobs listed even before the Andersons office opens. Some of those have been phoned in over the weekend and then emailed through to him the previous night, while others have come direct to his phone from individual farmers who know he does this run. Some jobs will arrive during the morning, and he's anticipating a busy day – usually the first day after a bank holiday is 'mayhem', whatever the weather. An average day for Andersons would be between 150 and 200 call-outs. Last bank holiday, it had 400.

And of course it's been an odd year. A malignant winter, receding and then advancing, flickering and deliberate, treacherous as a virus. Once lambing did get under way, some farms experienced losses of 30 or 40 per cent, and for the past few months Andersons has been run off its feet. The slow winter held the spring back until the light blazed in, and a great spring tide of daffodils and roses, snowdrops and celandines, narcissi and anemones came ripping over the countryside, foaming over themselves, reaching into everything all together and all at once. This is the quickening, the first bright fuse of life, though that sudden spring-lit growth can bring its own hazards. The best grass is steady-growing stuff, not this overnight traffic-light switch from brown to green rising so fast from the ground it leaves the nutrients behind.

As we drive, Ian talks. The trouble with bank holidays, he says, is that there's always a backlog. Some farmers will phone in stock when they discover it, but others will wait until the Tuesday. Sometimes they don't even discover a dead animal until several days later. Sometimes animals expire in plain view, but often a beast which knows it's going to die will do so in private – limp into the undergrowth, find a corner by the hawthorn, vanish into the scrub. Sometimes a quick headcount reveals the absence, sometimes it doesn't. Some farmers prefer to stack up a few dead before calling the knackerman, even though they know Andersons prefers fresh stock, and would rather go out six times to pick up six recently dead ewes from a farm than once to collect six rotting carcasses. It makes no difference to the cost, after all – prices are per animal, not per mile.

The first pick-up is a couple of ewes. We pull into the yard and though I can't spot anything Ian sees them immediately, sagging from a disused wooden trailer and covered with a feed sack. No farmer around, no one in the yard. He lowers the back of the tipper, pulls the winch from its hook, loops it round one of the ewes' forelegs and presses the button on the remote. The ewe bumps up the ramp and vanishes into the back, the action so mechanical it's difficult now to imagine her as something that once moved differently. Ian walks up behind her, unloops the winch, shuts the back, signs the form and leaves it tucked into the handlebars of a derelict quad. And then we're out of there, fast enough that the smell of rotting sheep doesn't hit us until we stop to let another car pass. 'We're in and out like the SAS. Most farmers don't even know we've been.'

Only in winter does he ever phone beforehand to give notice of his arrival. If it's been a long day and he turns up unannounced in the falling rain at 9 p.m. to a farm in total darkness, 'then the first I'm likely to know about it is a 12-bore against the side of my head. Most farmers don't take kindly to men with trucks wandering around their buildings at dead of night.'

But they phoned the job in, surely?

'And that was two days ago, and they've been that busy they've completely forgotten.'

As we pull away, a call comes in. It's a farmer called Lloyd Ian knows.

'I've got a ram here been fighting, and he's not won,' says Lloyd.

'Right,' says Ian, tapping the job in. 'There in half an hour.'

There follow a couple more farms in quick succession – three more sheep, one with its neck gnawed out by a fox or a dog. Another has been lying for several days and has blown up like a rubber glove. The stink of death drifts over the yard. No one in sight, and the weekend's rain lying dark in the tracks. Instead of attaching the winch to the ewe's legs as usual, Ian puts it round the neck. As the sheep bumps up the ramp the fleece slides off in clumps. The colour of the skin beneath is cold, sick, viscous with decay.

The truck comes swaggering down the ruts to another small Worcestershire farm, a scramble of old brick buildings. Even from a distance, there's an impression of love and cheap repairs, and a garden out the front roped with yellow roses. This time, both farmers are there – a mother and daughter, blonde and vigorous.

'Morning!' says the mother as Ian pulls himself down. The two of them come up close, their collies grinning. They know

Ian well – every farmer gets to know the slaughterman (and it is generally a job for the men) a little too well for comfort. Where there's livestock, there's dead stock, so the saying goes (Bert: 'I bloody hate that phrase'), and though any farmer with animals accepts a percentage of losses every year, that doesn't mean they don't feel a scratching unease at each one.

'It's one of my tiddlers today,' says the mother, tipping her head at the two twiggy lambs, all fluff and knuckles, that Ian is lifting into the back. 'Little one's been looking poorly for a couple of days. I told him to get on and die, but he didn't make up his mind until this morning.'

They offer tea and would clearly be happy to chat, but Ian does the forms, passes them over and jumps back into the cab. 'Sorry,' he calls through the window, restarting the engine, 'Busy morning.'

Some drivers, he explains as he turns his way back up the track, will stop. Farmers may not see anyone else but family or leave the farm for days on end, so the arrival of a familiar face is at least a chance to exchange a few practicalities, complain about the weather, share fragments of a day. Ian rarely lingers. 'I don't like stopping,' he says. 'I like going, and I like getting the job done.'

Back on the road the sun is out and the Worcestershire countryside is velvet green. A wave of cow parsley froths in our wake, and an uproar of birdsong greets us every time we step out of the cab. The next farm we go to is tucked round the back of an industrial unit. There are a lot of places like this – farms where the diversification plan has overwhelmed the original business. In some, we're still driving into a yard settled down into its own land, but others are lost or disguised. What looks like Tiny Toes Nursery or Beechcroft Leisure & Beauty now has a farm stuck shyly behind it. Past the false trail of new buildings ('Hillview Executive 3-, 4- and 5-Bed Fine & Country

Homes, Sunrise Solar & Biomass, Clee Architectural Salvage')
is a track sagged with use and a set of buildings designed not
to make an impression.

When we arrive at Ian's call-out, there's no sign of either
the farmer or the dead animal. As Ian parks, a small, weary
man in overalls with a face lined like foolscap appears round
the back of a shed. He is pushing a dead tup in a wheelbarrow.
The tup is upside down, legs dangling and head askew. His
horns are crowned with a ragged circle of cleavers and his balls
and stomach have turned blue.

'Fighting,' says Lloyd, bringing the barrow to rest.

'I can see,' says Ian.

'Went round them all last night and he was fine. Nothing
wrong with him, and then when I come round this morning, dead.
No warning, nothing. Picked a scrap and got his neck broke.'

'He's not that old,' says Ian.

'Two year,' says Lloyd. 'Paid £500 for him eight months ago.'

Ian takes the handles of the barrow. As it passes, Lloyd
watches it.

How have things been? I ask.

'Difficult,' says Lloyd.

Ian comes back out of the tipper and puts the empty barrow
down. 'Been a hard year for everyone.'

A silence.

'Busy morning?' says Lloyd.

'Fifteen, twenty.'

'We was just picking ourselves up again when the snow
came. Hit us right in the middle of lambing.'

Ian hands him the forms. Lloyd looks sightlessly for a
moment at the ticked boxes ('Ram, under 48 months'), and
puts his signature beneath it.

Ian swings himself back into the cab.

For the first time Lloyd looks up. 'You see us looking

cheerful for Andersons,' he says to me. 'But I tell you, half the time we're smiling through the tears.'

'Not your fault,' says Ian.

'Maybe,' says Lloyd, 'but the point is to get the bloody things to market and get them sold. After that they can die all they like.'

By the time we're halfway down the track, Lloyd has disappeared.

'Poor man,' says Ian as we pass the enterprise park, and then changes the subject. His view of sheep ('Keel over if you so much as look at them the wrong way') is not a minority one. Among those who manage the lowland breeds the general view is that a sheep's main aim once in the world is to get out of it as fast as possible. They cast themselves or they fight or they get scab or bluetongue or they overheat or they eat the wrong grass or they find the one rusty nail in a clean field or they get stressed by horses or dogs or a change in the weather, or they eat yew or they get infected cuts after shearing or they abort their own lambs or they've got too much of one mineral but not enough of another. Bert: 'If a sheep could, it'd die twice.'

Once back out on the road Ian drives fast, competently, taking the narrow single-track lanes around Worcestershire with styleless efficiency. That was what got him into this job – not the knackering, but the driving. His father died when Ian was three months old and his mother wasn't able to look after him, so it was his grandparents who brought him up. His granddad was a knackerman, so Ian started doing the rounds with him from a young age. He left school at fifteen, knowing that what he really wanted to do was be a rally driver – 'that's my first love' – but also that there was no money in it. Or rather, that there was plenty of money in it, but it was all going in the wrong direction.

On the other hand, he was already trained as a slaughter-man and had also realised that knackering would at least allow him to spend a lot of time on the road. Did he need qualifications? No, not when he learned. His granddad taught him everything he knew, and 'then the Ministry came and checked on me once I'd shown I'd killed everything in sight – pigs, goats, cattle, sheep, horses. And that was it. Qualified.'

As with the rest of farming, knackering doesn't go in for euphemism. Andersons' animals don't get euthanised or put down or put to sleep, they don't go to heaven or depart this world or pass away or pop their clogs or kick the bucket. They aren't even culled. They die, and sometimes Ian kills them.

'We're just dustmen,' he says. 'Dustmen for dead animals.'

Dustmen they may be, but they're dustmen with autonomy. Andersons lets its experienced drivers set their own routes and work out their own hours. He is sixty now and has been doing this job his whole working life. He has a partner but no children, a dog, a car he sometimes still rallies, a house that's been paid for, and enough put away that he has no need to keep working. He does it, he says, 'Because I love it. I enjoy my job and I get paid to do it. If they let me, I'd work Christmas.'

What does he love about it? 'The driving.'

Apart from the driving?

'The driving.' He inclines his head. 'And the planning. Working it all out. What route, how the jobs all join up, being out here. Being my own boss.'

And the killing? 'I do it because I have to do it. It's part of the job. I don't particularly like it but it's there.'

There are, he explains, two ways of doing it. He is a licensed slaughterman, which means he uses a captive bolt gun pressed directly against the crown of the animal's head, which fires a bolt straight into the brain, killing it instantly. But when dealing with an animal out in the wild or terrified of humans

31

or crazy with pain, Andersons has a group of trained riflemen who shoot from a distance. If they can, they clear the area beforehand, since nothing makes an animal seem more alive than the moment of its death. Deer scatter. Cows buck. Pigs have hard skulls. And horses, it is generally conceded, are worst of all. Nobody likes doing horses, because the owners get upset and want to stay and hold the collar, and the slaughterman gets nervous, and sod's law dictates that after thirty jobs that all went without a hitch it will be at that exact moment that the horse puts its head up or pulls away or just looks at them with one infinite brown eye before ripping through its halter and running for the hills.

The riflemen need a gun licence and specialist training, and though some of the Andersons staff are both slaughter-men and riflemen Ian doesn't use a rifle and doesn't want to. During the foot-and-mouth crisis in 2001 he remained as a driver, not a slaughterman, still picking up the regular jobs. Even in the midst of the worst epidemic for a generation, Andersons still had to deal with the ordinary work of agricul-tural life and death. All that changed for him was that every job was a single one (pick-up and return to depot) to avoid cross-contamination. At points he was lifting whole herds from farms – places where the DEFRA vets (or MAFF, as it then was) had been in and shot them all. By the end they were shooting so many that MAFF itself supposedly got a bit trigger-happy with the qualifications. 'It was, "Can you stand up? Can you hold a gun?" They were meant to check people were licensed, but they couldn't shoot fast enough.'

The disease brought some strange characters rattling out of the woodwork. Even now Andersons occasionally gets people applying for the job who are a bit odd around firearms, just a little too interested in shooting. They're easy enough to spot, and they get weeded out quickly.

So what qualities do you need for this job?

'God!' says Ian. 'Never thought about it. You know the wrong 'uns when you see them, but it's hard to put your finger on.' He slows for a UPS van. 'There's lots that don't take to it.' The UPS van speeds up again. 'Patience. Patience, definitely.'

Patience in dealing with farmers: a rare breed, singular as pangolins. Patience in knowing the habits of each one, and how they're likely to behave when their animals die. There are those who show nothing on the outside but then take their anger out on the knackerman, those who neglect their own stock, those who take each small loss as a break to their own hearts.

And experience. Experience in reading an animal's physiognomy and anticipating how it will behave – ears forward, eyes hot with fear, or the ones which look docile but then rear or strike the bolt gun from his hand. Animals – cows in particular – will read people, and even when Ian parks the tipper where they can't see it they will sense the morbidity on him.

'You get that dead smell, and they don't like it. Doesn't matter what you do, how much you disinfect, they can always smell it on you.'

He's been caught out a couple of times. Once, a few years ago, he had a cow with a broken leg. He and the farmer were concentrating so hard on getting the cow penned into a corner of the field that neither of them realised the rest of the herd were close behind them. The farmer was crushed against the fencing and had his arm broken, and Ian felt lucky to have escaped with just bruises.

And animal behaviour is changing. Or rather, animals are the same but the farming practices around them have altered, which means the way animals respond to them has also changed. A smaller workforce and a bigger herd (or flock), indoor parlours, calves separated from their mothers and brought up with artificial weaners, sows raised in farrowing pens ... Where once a farmer might have known every Daisy and Buttercup in his herd, they're now lucky to remember a few bright characters in an entirely black-and-white cast: Tag number 43267 is slow into the milkers, 59789 spooks easily, 41390 has a slight drag to the left fore.

At least dairy cows are usually in close proximity to humans twice a day – the milkers need to be attached or new cows shown where to go – but beef cattle may not be used to handling, and what contact they do have may either be painful (injections, bovine tuberculosis reactor tests) or frightening (into pens, up and down lorry ramps). It's like pets with vets: no animal in its right mind would cheerfully submit to the bewilderment of human processes, to having its teeth groped or its neck needled or a hand rammed up its bottom. Small wonder, therefore, that the final human interaction is no longer met with docility, but crazed, rodeoing panic.

'You always look for your exits, you always make sure you're near the door,' says Ian. He always insists on a crush (a metal stall) and at least one other person to help him – 'If the farmer says "She's in there", but he won't go in himself, or if you walk in and the farmer shuts the door behind you, you've got a problem. Because if he won't go in there with the animal, then ...' He grimaces. 'Amazing the number who try and pull that one on you.'

Does he consider himself an animal lover?

'Oh, yes,' he says. 'I kill animals all day every day, but I still cry like a baby when I take my dog to the vet. My old dog had diabetes and she was old and it weren't going to get better, and I knew what the sensible thing to do was. But could I? It took me weeks to make that appointment. I cried from the moment I went in the door to the moment I left.'

Certain jobs, he hates. Racehorses in particular – if a horse isn't winning, the owner or trainer will often insist it is killed rather than sold on. Animals which have somehow escaped onto motorways, railway lines, down embankments, into ponds or canals or rivers. Some are the victims of barn or stable fires. Some rip themselves to shreds on barbed wire fences, are burned or electrocuted or impale themselves on railings. None of them are easy, and in the case of animals which are insured, the owner will often insist that Ian waits around for the vet to arrive, because it needs that official signature before a claim can be made. He does not like standing around beside an animal in distress waiting for a piece of paper.

Which leads him on to another subject – the strangest jobs he's ever had. Over the years Andersons has done everything from minke whales to zebras. ('We get tigers and lions,' says Ian's boss Will Anderson later. 'We had a hippo. Bless them, they just go in a skip.') They also occasionally pick up from a nearby safari park. 'Everything,' says Ian. 'Everything you can think of. There was a giraffe once.' It had died of natural causes, but 'God, that was tricky. First we couldn't get it out of the giraffe house and then we couldn't get it in the back of the tipper. It took us ages to work it out. Took a lot of folding, I can tell you.'

It's early afternoon now. The transmitter crackles and then goes silent again.

Five minutes later, we pull into another farmyard. The animal to be slaughtered is a newborn calf, a Friesian. He was born yesterday evening and is standing now, still lovely and precarious, in an improvised pen near the edge of the shed. He is speckled with glossy black splodges and his ears are pricked and trusting. There's absolutely nothing wrong with him. But this farm is under a bTB restriction, which means that until the herd is retested, found to be clear and the restriction lifted, none of these bull calves can be sold on the open market. A dairy herd needs only cows, and many farms can't afford to rear animals for free.

Together Ian and Rob, the farmer, lead the calf out into the shed. Ian has on a pair of thick rubber gloves and his bolt gun. He holds the calf by the chin, butts its head up against the side of his leg for support, presses the gun to the crown of the calf's head and pulls the trigger. The calf, pulling back a little from Ian's grip, falls instantly, hind legs jolting. Ian pushes the blue plastic pithing rod through the hole in the calf's skull and down the back, severing the nerves and the spinal cord. For a few moments longer the calf's muscles continue to spasm. Then he lies still, a thin line of blood trickling out of that perfect hole.

Unnoticed by us, the other cows have come up and are standing in a line, watching. The calf is out in the open and they are near the sheds, separated from him by a thin strand of electric wire. The cows' heads are down and their ears are flicking back and forward, slightly stepped back. Beneath their soft lashes their gaze moves from us to the calf and to us again. One cow turns her head away and nudges the neck of another. The calf lies there on the strawless yard in front of them, black and white. And red.

Rob stands by the tipper. In theory he could probably have done this job himself. Like most farmers, he has a licence and a shotgun and the legal right to shoot any animal in distress. But the vast majority of farmers don't. Not only because after the BSE outbreak they can no longer bury or incinerate dead animals on the farm, but because farmers do not want to destroy their own animals. They might be rearing them for meat and they absolutely understand that their ultimate destination is an abattoir, but that doesn't mean they like killing. No farmer really wants to see the knackerman, and no one wants to pay the £95 it costs to dispose of a cow or the £17 for a sheep. It's the same as Ian's old dog: they could do it themselves, but they can't.

Rob, like Lloyd, must be in his late fifties; small, stocky, tight. He stands beside me, squinting, his back to the calf. If I wasn't here he would have found some minor job – moving a gate, a bit more straw – which would allow him to turn away from Ian and the moment of destruction. While the bTB restriction remains in force on the farm Rob's cattle can only be sold to other farms in a similar situation, thus giving him even less opportunity to justify keeping bull calves. Got to be done, he says, like he must have said a thousand times before, just can't make it work financially, reasonable rule and all, another twenty-four days to run before the sixty-day gap is up and they're all hoping to go free ... But it's clear from the angle of his body and the set of his face that even though all of this is true and the sort of thing you say to yourself every time it happens, it doesn't make it better.

The calf slides up the ramp behind him.

'A farmer's job is to look after animals,' Rob says finally. 'To feed them, take care of them, make sure they're all right. It's not his job to kill the healthy ones.' He stands for a second. Then he moves away.

'I don't have a problem killing an animal in distress,' Ian says, driving away. 'I really don't. The quicker it's done, the better. I don't want to see things in pain – I want to get it over with as quick as possible. The times I have a problem, it's killing healthy animals.' He is still taken up with bTB. 'There's a lot of it round here,' he says. 'Big chunk of my work.'

Coming to a T-junction, he slows, pointing out a line of bloated mattresses and rubble bags in the spring grass.

'Fly-tippers. That's the bank holiday – that stuff weren't there Friday.'

Because councils are now charging for the removal and disposal of rubbish, people are circumventing the payments by dumping rubbish illegally, often on farmland. It then falls to the farmer to deal with the resulting mess. Recently, an increasing number of old or sick horses are also being stranded or let loose in strange fields at quiet times of night. Fly-grazing is the same as fly-tipping: owners may no longer want the horse, but can't afford – or don't want – to pay the charges for having them legally slaughtered, so they let them out to starve or take their chances.

Ian resumes. 'One TB job, I had to shoot a hundred and forty infected pedigree cattle in an afternoon. There was so many I couldn't do it all myself – we had to bring in a couple of extra guys to help.' Any farm which has over a certain number of reactors has its whole herd condemned. 'That, I hated, I really hated. I did the job, same as always, but I got to tell you, I took extra care – if you've got to do something like that you want it done quick, no issues. That farmer had spent his whole lifetime building up this pedigree herd, getting the bloodstock just right. He had a couple of reactors and next thing someone from the Ministry tells him he has to get rid of the lot. They all went in a day. One single day: the whole lot, every cow. How that man wasn't hanging from a tree the next day, I do not know, I really don't. He was distraught. Just distraught.'

The next job is a larger farm up on the side of a ridge. This time, it's a cow with a broken leg. The access is difficult, so Ian reverses the tipper into the yard, the back end beeping as he does so. In the farmhouse garden there are children's toys, coffee mugs on the table, an abandoned towel. A Volvo XC60 with one door still open stands at the end of the track, and inside the house there's the churn of a food mixer. Ian goes to the garden gate and calls hello a couple of times. Nothing. The mixer stops. Silence. He rings the bell. The silence gets louder.

'Leave them,' Ian says. 'Can you get the gate?'

Through the yard past the silage and the rutted field, the cow is in a field on her own. She is lying awkwardly over on one side, her udder bagging over uncomfortably. She's a brown

Friesian, soft-eyed, the broken bone raised beneath her skin like a wrong answer. It's clear from the flattened marks on the grass that she has been here for a while, dragging herself down the field. Some farmers will leave animals who seem ill or are injured for a couple of days before they call Andersons. They hope they will recover. Or that, by dying, the animal will have made the decision for them.

As Ian approaches the cow sits up, ears forward. I have no proof of this, but I know she knows what's coming. Again, Ian walks up to her, no hesitation, and takes hold of one of her horns. She lowers her head a little, a slight, generous offering. He puts the captive bolt to her crown and then he shoots. In one short motion she rolls over onto her side, broken leg banging against the empty air.

The bolt has made almost no sound but, as if on some kind of silent timer, the farmer appears. He is tall, mid-sixties, and his daughter is with him. The daughter goes off in search of the telehandler and I look at the cow, the subtle shifts in tone and hue, her great dark eye already blurring out of reach. She is so huge, so factual, such a complete being. The daughter reappears in the telehandler and the cow is lifted by her hobbled legs out of the field, gravity dragging at her. The chat is minimal.

Out on the road, it takes an effort to speak. What will happen to her? What happens to an undiseased but injured cow once it's shot?

'Cat two,' says Ian.

What's that?

In bureaucratic terms, he explains, she's Category 2, easily recyclable: both her hide and her meat are good. Back at the depot she will be skinned, the hide will be taken by tanners for leather, and her meat will be sold on to hunts or safari parks or pet food manufacturers. Category 1 is the stuff you can't do anything with – the stinky sheep in the back of the tipper, the animals over forty-eight months old.

In the past a dead animal had a use and thus a financial value. There are still older farmers who remember the days when the knackers paid them, not the other way round. Bone was fertiliser, meat was food, fat was candles, fleece was wool and hide was leather. Now, most of those uses have gone. The cost of shearing a sheep usually exceeds the price for the wool and dead sheep rot so quickly they're all just dumped and rendered. Horses aren't used much. Their hides are too thin for leather and most have had so many injections they cannot even be classified as pet food. All Category 1 animals are taken back to Andersons, placed in sealed containers, and left for the renderers to pick up, and the Category 2 meat goes either to local hunts or to the safari parks; lambs fed to lions.

It used to be that when dead animals were incinerated the resulting black ash was mixed with bitumen and used as road surfacing. Tallow became candles, horns and hooves were made into containers or utensils or boiled down for glue. The BSE outbreak in the late 1990s changed all that. New regulations outlawed the old 'dead pits' where farmers would dump carcasses. Now, every animal had to be collected and taken off the farm. Small abattoirs were closed down or issued with such an onerous list of improvements and requirements they went out of business. Fallen-stock operators either fell in line with the new testing regulations or went solo below the radar, or stopped trading. And, most importantly, the finances reversed. Where once a dead horse or bull at least had the value the knacker would pay, now it's another cost.

'Used to be,' says Ian, 'we paid them and the renderers paid us. Now the farmers pay us and we pay the renderers.'

At the moment it's Andersons' biggest outgoing – £100 per ton to the renderers: more than fuel or maintenance or the charges DEFRA makes for inspections. The renderers in their turn are taking what they describe as 'commercial waste', cooking it up and making it into biodiesel or protein. It is in theory entirely possible that we could one day run cars off dead chickens.

By this time it's mid-afternoon and every time we stop at a junction or pause to let another car pass, the sweet morbid reek of those dead sheep comes surging forward, thick enough to seem almost visible. Watching the wing mirrors I see the drivers behind us closing up their windows and a man driving the school bus recoil, squinting with displeasure. If it wasn't for getting to a farm on the edge of Bridgnorth, Ian would usually avoid towns. Over the years he's developed his own customised circuit of anonymous country lanes, a private system of ring roads round every built-up area which allows him to keep the smell a safe 25 yards behind him. Once in a while, he'll get a pick-up like this and be unable to avoid going through the centre.

'That's embarrassing – I'm stuck in the middle of Tenbury or something and all the schoolkids choking and pointing and waving their arms in front of their faces.' It's other peoples' reactions which bother Ian, not his own. He's been at this job so long that death is just the smell of work to him. 'I don't even notice,' he admits. 'Once in a while I'll get to a job and the farmer will say something, and it didn't even occur to me. It does get a bit much in summer, to be fair, but it's not usually bad as long as I keep going.'

Oddly enough, the thing that really makes him gag is chickens. In the past decade or so poultry has become big business, and the number of units are increasing year on year, thousands upon thousands of chickens reared in huge sheds under audited conditions. Andersons now has several lorries just doing day-in, day-out pick-ups – the binned victims of heat-related epidemics or the everyday attrition of thirty-eight-day rotations. 'This time of year, because it's getting warm again, their fans pack in, they have problems, so they have mass killings, freezers go down. A couple of years ago we had four lorries just doing disasters off chicken farms. We were taking stuff off the renderers. They were passing it back to us because they couldn't cope with the volume.'

Two more farms, the first a tiny place where a heifer is laid under sacking in a shed, the final one a big dairy where there's a dead cow round the back and a live calf which had tangled a back leg in the bars of the pen, snapping the femur. That was three days ago, and the leg has now swollen to twice its healthy size. This time the calves are all on their own, penned in a line in a long low byre in strawed wooden enclosures with buckets outside. The calves can see past the bars and watch us, silent and swivel-eared, as the herdsman picks out the calf, brings it down the line and holds it for Ian. The captive bolt makes a click like the latch on a gate, but the watching calves still roll and flatten with fear, stepping towards the backs of their pens as the herdsman carries the calf out to the tipper.

This place is big, with a Thai restaurant at the front in the old farmhouse and a huddle of signboards by the entrance pointing the way to businesses round the back: pet grooming, software upgrades, satellite phone services. The next has sagged wooden joists, windows patched with feed sacks and a rewilded Ford Focus growing dandelions by the silage clamp. The whole place has a general air of defeat, as if the buildings themselves are subsiding with exhaustion, now too tired to do anything but keep going.

If I wanted a random overview of farming, I couldn't have picked better if I'd drawn straws. Some of the places we've been to were huge corporate successes overgrazing the margins and doing clever things with dairy or plastic. Some yards are scrupulous, others seem barely habitable. In a tiny smallholding at the end of a suburban lane (live ewe, disease) there's a man standing in shorts and flip-flops chopping up window architraves with a rusty open-bladed table saw while a family of ginger kittens pounce round his feet. Others have a squared-off, military tidiness, a strictly disinfected sense of control. Some places park the harvests of the most recent refinancing (new Ford Ranger pick-ups, cloudless Discoverys) on the gravel out front, or escort the visitor to the farm office along a recently planted driveway of chestnuts. In others, it takes a genuine effort to work out which is the farmhouse and which the byre.

It's past 5 p.m. now and the loop is taking us back towards the border. At the depot Ian drives the tipper into the big shed at the back, sorts the carcasses out into different categories and sluices the whole lot out while I go to find the manager.

Will Anderson is the fourth generation of this family to do this job. He's early thirties, good-natured, bearded, with a series of tattoos poking out from under his shirt, including a delicate blue-edged feather down his left forearm. Invincibly cheerful, he's only recently taken over the family business from his father Robert. Andersons was started almost exactly 100 years ago by his great-great-grandfather, who came back from the First World War and started taking scrap wool and pelts, 'the stuff nobody else wanted'. Having bought a horse and cart, Michael began taking dead cattle to sell on to abattoirs and started trading in hides. At one stage, Andersons had four different yards around the Midlands, but after BSE they were forced to shut down for a while. They scaled back, consolidating everything into the depot here, upgraded the buildings and did what was required to conform to the new legislation.

The 2001 foot-and-mouth outbreak, coming so soon after BSE, proved 'the thing that kept us going, really'.

Will himself never thought he'd be doing this job. Knackering was definitely not his cup of tea: 'Dead animals don't do anything for me.' When he was young he wanted to be a vet. Then he went to live with his mother in Bristol and got himself a degree in graphic design, but in 2008 the recession hit, so he came over to Wales for a year to help sort things out. He has been here ever since.

Will is licensed as a rifleman and will go out to an emergency in the middle of the night if he has to, but 'I don't like it. It's not my thing – that's why I'm in here. I like the interaction with the farmers, I like the interaction with the drivers. That's the main thing to me, that's what's most important: that everybody's happy.'

And there are benefits to being a known quantity. Because it's a family business and there are so many family farms round here, he must get places where he's fourth-generation, the farmer is seventh-generation, they've been using Andersons for a century …?

'Yeah, but sometimes it's the other way as well: my great-granddad fell out with their great-granddad and nobody's ever used us again, and they just live up the road – it's crazy. They're probably calling us every name under the sun because my granddad shorted them 10p years ago.'

The upside – if you can call it that – is a very close-knit group of people and a line of work that isn't going to run out any time soon. Which gives Andersons a ringside glimpse of an industry shifting. A lot of their customers are the old boys, the breadline farmers whose sons have looked up from their lives and realised there are jobs in this world which have days off.

'The way it's going, farming is diverging. You're either getting someone who's got ten sheep or they've got three thousand.

There's not as many in the middle. The big farms, I think they're very much "stock". And then at the other end there's a lot of hobby farmers coming in. They're a bit clueless, really, as to the way it is. Because they're coming from cities, they don't really know about farming at all, and it's like, "I got a sheep here", and it'll be down three fields away, and I got to send a 3.5 ton lorry …' He grins. ' … Hang on.' He dives out of the office and returns a moment later with a piece of cardboard in a frame. On it is written: '<u>Andersons:</u> *Animal through this gate, then through gate and through stream. Keep left to bottom of field, through gate into next field, keep left alongside of stream. Animal by tree. Thanks a lot. Please shut gates*.' The board is usually displayed in the reception area as a tribute to difficult customers.

Will sits down again. 'The old isolated farms are the trickiest to get away from,' he resumes, 'because they're the ones who want to talk, but they tend to be the ones who'll leave a sheep here and a cow there, and you have to go round and hump down the fallen stock because they haven't got a farm manager. But the only difference between the small and the big farms is that the small farms you tend to be talking to the boss, and the bigger farms you're talking to a manager or a stockman.'

And everyone, large or small, has had a tough start to the year. 'This spring has been very, very busy – the busiest spring we've ever had. Been absolutely manic. Started to get busy mid-February and we're still busy now. When we had that bad snow we were closed for two days, we went out on the Sunday and collected about ten cows, and then on the Monday we had about fifty-five cows. It's just been non-stop. You expect cows this time of year, because you get the grass growing quick and they get mineral deficiencies and start fitting and pass away. So we expect that. But we don't expect sheep.'

So a lot of animals aren't as resistant as they had been in the past?

'No. When we had that snow before [in 2014], we had a lot of stock, and then we had a quiet summer because what's left were all stronger, more resilient. And you've got better stock from that. You go to markets and the stock's worth more because there's less of it. It does sort of counterbalance itself.'

And does the job still get to him? Yes, he says, and no. 'It's like in hospitals – people laughing and joking, black humour. We do become a little bit numb to it – you appreciate what you're doing but you do become a bit cold. It becomes a very normal procedure, so you become used to going in, shooting the animal, getting the animal on and ...' He tails off. 'The most difficult ones are definitely bull calves. Everyone in this place hates doing bull calves. Worst bit is that they really remind you of dogs, because they're only little things. There's literally nothing wrong with them – you're just doing it for the good of the farm, really. They're just dead weight.'

Downstairs in the big shed, the tipper has been disinfected and the bodies have been sorted. Lined against the wall are a stack of biosecure plastic boxes used for storing the stock that can't be picked up immediately. In one area there's a line of fresh samples. In a separate bay a neat pile of fresh cow hides lies in a corner, a sack of salt beside them. The hides will be taken by tanners to be turned into shoes or car seats, the bTB samples sent to DEFRA to condemn or not to condemn.

Driving back after Ian has dropped me, the day doesn't prompt any big thoughts, only a kind of dry exhaustion. I think of the depot at the end. Ranged across the wet concrete floor below the white lights are the cows and calves Ian and the other drivers picked up today, the calves splayed around the big brown Friesian in the middle. If I didn't think it would be seen as sentimental, I would go and touch the brown cow, say goodbye to her. I wish I had.

2

Rise

When I first arrived at the cottage in October 2013 Bert and Alison were still running the farm. Bert was then seventy-six and Alison in her mid-sixties, and the farm had been ticking along unhappily for a long while – 300 sheep, 180 acres, a father and son who passed each other several dozen times a day but never met each other's eye. Through the thick of a morning gale I would hear the chug of the quad bike and watch Bert hauling back up the field with a ewe or a bale slung over its wide red haunch. Whatever the time or emergency, Bert always took things at the same pace – low gear, low throttle, a fat wake of diesel smoke trailed over the field's edge back towards the track, a lamb sometimes gripped within the folds of his jacket.

When he wasn't carrying anything, Bryn or Come Here would ride pillion. The two dogs lived for the morning round, and would be standing by the door of the kennel long before Bert came out from breakfast. Setting out, they'd leap onto the bike and arrange themselves in the manner of family crests – *House sigil, quartered; dog, pursuivant; wolf, fanged, rampant* – according to a long-settled pecking order, Bryn to the left, Come Here to the right. Both of them liked to stand straight-legged on the bumpy bits, whiskers blazing, knowing their role was to bestow gravitas on the meanest of farm tasks and generally considering themselves far too important even to bark.

In truth, Come Here was a terrible sheepdog. Lazy, unfocused, addicted to sex and theft. Issued with an instruction, he talked back. Whistled up, he'd feign deafness or sit at the top of the field with the breeze caressing his fur, a thousand-yard look in his eye. It was easy to imagine him with sunglasses in a movie. He was iffy with chickens: there had been incidents (attributed, for diplomacy's sake, to foxes) involving the discovery of feathers in odd places. The way he sat outside their cage and watched as they took their morning corn suggested less an avuncular concern for their ongoing welfare than dinner, unplucked. If Bert was moving the sheep on his own, Come Here might remain long enough to get them through the gate and onto the lane before vanishing at the critical moment, more interested in passing the time of day with a visiting terrier. Bert – left to cover both ends of the flock with only Bryn for assistance – would shout himself scarlet but it made no difference. Come Here came when he wanted to but didn't when he didn't. Late in the summer evenings I'd often see the shape of a dog outlined on the peak of the hill heading towards the village, a stubborn set to his shoulders. There was an attractive young retriever bitch in one of the far houses who had recently come into heat. He wasn't the only suitor, but he was very persistent.

Bert cursed him out with the same thoroughness he cursed his son. But he needed two dogs, and as things stood he didn't have time for training up a young one. The only alternative was either Alison, who had plenty of work of her own, or their neighbour, Low-Output Llew. Every morning there was the morning tour, Bert's daily survey of all the tasks added to a perpetually lengthening must-do list: lame ewe, broken-hinged gate, ice in trough, hay to unbale, hedge to patch. Sometimes it took an hour, sometimes – with Come Here's assistance – it took five. The circuit might change in shape and the tasks might expand or contract, but Bert had lived the whole passage of his life according to the facts of this landscape and the insistence of the list, a benign unrelenting cycle on which he could stake more lives than just his own.

Lately, however, Bert had barely been into most of the sheds. For the last few months he'd had enough energy to get angry but none for a fight. What he needed was to rest in the house, and what he wanted was excuses to get out of that house. David had returned from Spain and, until he found a flat of his own, Bert, Alison and David were living together. It wasn't easy. David did his best to help with the farm work, but he kept different hours – partly deliberately, so he wouldn't have to share duties with his father. The two remained as separate to one another as far foreign land.

Bert would come down to the cottage, have a cup of tea, tell stories. Many of those stories involved Ron Gifford. Ron was thirty years older than Bert, born somewhere in the middle of twelve children and lived his whole life in the little cottage one field further up the hill. Three of his brothers were killed during the First World War, and by the time Ron was eleven a further two of the older ones were already out to work.

One day his father came to pick him up from school. The two of them walked a few miles to one of the neighbouring farms. The farmer stood up from his work and looked at the boy. 'B'ain't very big, is it?'

'Big enough.'

'Can it work?'

'Raised to it.'

'Seven shillings.'

'Eight.'

A desultory haggle.

'Sunday,' said his father to Ron by way of farewell. 'Don't make trouble.'

From then on Ron worked six and a half days a week. On Sunday afternoons he walked back over the fields and paid his wages over to his parents. During the week he slept in the hay barn and ate pork fat. The farm had only large pigs, all white, no lean meat on them since, as Bert put it, the old farmer was, 'an absolute bugger for fat bacon'. Ron started off hating the taste; by the end of six weeks, he ate nothing else.

The experience taught Ron all there was to know about both people and animals. Over the years most of his family moved away, but Ron stayed and started his own smallholding, which in time became a larger one. When it got taken out by the 1967 outbreak of foot-and-mouth he restocked with only a few animals and went back to doing contract work for others, including Bert's dad Gerwyn. He learned to drive, but though he travelled all over the county he preferred the work he could get at home.

Down the hill at Rise, Gerwyn refused to pay Bert a wage or give him enough time off the farm to earn money elsewhere. Bert had started trying to provide himself with an income by breeding pigs. But the harder Bert worked, the harder Gerwyn worked him. The pigs, he said, were a distraction, and if Bert wanted to keep them he could only spend time on them at the end of the day after the rest of his farm work was done. Even getting up earlier and going to bed later, Bert was finding it almost impossible to manage both farm and pigs. Ron was a generation older, but he sympathised with Bert and offered him a few free hours' help on the side. During haymaking he'd get back from his own work at 8 p.m. or so, then come down the hill to help Bert. It was the beginning of a profound – and mostly unspoken – friendship between the two men.

'One in a million,' said Bert. 'One in a million. Thing was, he weren't a great stockman – he worked too hard and too fast. But the kindest man I ever knew.'

In later years Ron kept a garden just so he could take round a handful of apples or gooseberries to anyone who might want them. He provided Bert with good nature and generosity when there was little of it around, acting as a mentor in all things for as long as he was physically able. The two men, older and younger, would work for hours side by side in the piggery, silent and steady. Bert grew to trust him in most things, and since – initially at least – Ron was offering his services for free, his father couldn't complain. The only thing Bert didn't take his advice on was anything to do with cars. 'He weren't a bad driver,' said Bert reasonably. 'It was just you didn't always know which side of the road he was going to pass you on.'

In truth, Bert's stories about Ron were a distraction, a self-soothing way of drawing himself away from all the things he found wrong. When the stories ran out he would return to the same sore points: David had no idea about farming ('heart's not in it'), no idea about land ('stupid notions'), no idea about looking after animals ('up too late'). He was no good with money or working away at a job you hated just because you had to ('workshy'). He was a dreamer, writing songs or stories, posting things on YouTube. He wanted to try suckler cows again or a different breed of sheep – 'Over my dead body'. He wanted to convert some of the old buildings into a B&B, grow more energy crops, rent out some of the grazing. He had been mollycoddled by his mother. He hadn't even had the sense to pick a decent wife. 'I won't stand for it. I. Will. Not. Stand. For it.'

Bert knew his own father had been a bastard to him, but he seemed unable to stop himself from hurting both himself and his son in his turn. Once in a while he would concede that David did have a knack for stock ('If you get a difficult lambing, he's better than me'), and had some valid ideas for the farm, even if they were ones he disagreed with. And even he could see that David loved the place as much as he did. And then he'd go back to the same complaints. Round and round, dragging and polluted, never mending, never clearing.

3

Succession

The meeting starts late. It's a low evening in September, quiet, pensive. It rained a couple of hours ago and the roads are liquorish with black light. The water on the beech trees flares in the sunset and in a neighbouring field a donkey brays.

Round the village hall car park there is still bunting strung up from the Harvest Supper. Once every few minutes a car approaches at speed and another Hilux or Trooper rushes in through the gateway, pulling up with a squeak of brakes and loosing a knot of farmers who head for the hall at a run. So sorry, they all say, shoving keys into handbags and phones onto silent: problem with the harvester/baler/car/babysitter/ alarm. Each of the little groups slows on the threshold and then walks over in the direction of the tea urn. At the back of the hall there's a table laid with a paper cloth and a homemade ginger cake, and for a couple of minutes they busy themselves with spoons and milk before standing looking out into the hall at everyone else doing the same. Their hands are in their pockets and each person has one foot half-turned towards the door.

The meeting still doesn't start. Quietly it becomes apparent that the lateness is deliberate – or, if not deliberate, then strategically beneficial. As the minutes wander past, those who recognise each other move from the refuge of the table to the centre of the room. The local NFU (National Farmers' Union) rep Clare Greener works her way round making introductions – one arable farmer to another, a vineyard to a hop farm, a dairy to a cheese press. The younger ones begin to pull away from the old. One man who has arrived on his own stands by the banner at the back of the room until he is eased into conversation with a woman of the same age. The more confident – the ones who have done this before – start moving from group to group, finding connections, shaking hands. The noise level increases.

Half an hour later everyone is seated at a table arranged in a horseshoe shape near the stage. At the front there's a woman standing by a whiteboard with a marker in her hand. This is the second part of a succession discussion organised by the NFU but run by Heather Wildman, one of a very small group of people in the UK who mediate between farming families. She works with them either individually or in groups like this, getting them to talk about the intractable and plan for the impossible.

Heather's job has only really existed in Britain for the past fifteen years or so, and even now there's a sense of novelty to it. In the past when things went wrong on a farm, lawyers dealt with the legal parts, accountants dealt with the finances, bureaucrats dealt with the regulations, but nobody dealt with the people. As she explains, she meets farmers who are on the brink of selling up/divorcing/shooting themselves/shooting each other, sits them down in a neutral space and gets them to talk about things they don't ever talk about.

Heather is mid-forties, warm smile, comfortable figure. She herself comes from a Cumbrian farming family, did a Nuffield farming scholarship, travelled widely and then, after more than two decades away, came back for an event. While there she came across several old friends who were still farming and, 'I was shocked. You look at agriculture and you see so many people who just look miserable.' Heather was drawn in, first as a consultant and then more broadly as a succession facilitator. As a business it took a while to build but people gradually began to see the persuasion in spending a few hundred pounds on a day's mediation instead of several thousand in lawyers' fees.

The sessions are split into two parts, with six months or so between first and second. At the first, each person has the chance to explain what the farm and the future looks like and outline – discreetly – some of the issues which might well have built up over time. They go away with homework to do, wills to be drawn up, handover plans to debate. This second meeting is as much to find out if those conversations actually happened as to move things along.

The issue which crops up most frequently is age. It remains one of the many paradoxes that, while the stock itself may be getting younger, farmers themselves are not. By every possible index the agricultural sector appears to be travelling in the opposite direction to the rest of the country. As Britain itself shifts into new shapes, farming – the industry which most defines this country's sense of itself – appears to be getting steadily smaller, worse paid, older, whiter, more masculine and more monocultural. At present, DEFRA doesn't even bother preparing statistics on the ethnic make-up of farming; there's no point. A 2017 report on workplace diversity by the right-wing Policy Exchange Forum put it down by diabolical. While nearly 40 per cent of doctors are from non-white backgrounds, only 1.4 per cent of farm workers are. DEFRA's survey of agricultural labour is produced every three or four years and the most recent one (2016) showed what most of farming already knew: over four-fifths (84 per cent) of farm 'holders' (owners or tenants) are male, and 40 per cent aged over sixty-five. Younger farmers (those under fifty) tended to be on larger farms, and were more concentrated in the pig and poultry sector. Within farming as a whole, only 2 per cent of holders are below the age of thirty-five.

The usual response to this statistic is to point out that the person whose name is on the farm deeds may well not be the person doing the farming. So it may be that the name belongs to someone who was born when ploughing was still done by horse, but it's actually his son, his daughter, his granddaughter, his niece, who is doing the actual physical work. In many cases this is true – the old boy has retired, put his feet up, is doing Great Things with the local Rotary Club, but often he's still in overalls. He may have a bad back, pins in every limb, a gammy leg (or two), a replacement hip (or two), high blood pressure, cataracts, a landfill liver, the first (or last) signs of dementia, he may be ten, twenty, thirty years beyond the age of retirement, but nothing and no one except an appointment with the Grim Reaper in person is going to stop him. One of the most moving and frustrating things about traditional family farming is that many farmers simply do not recognise the concept of retire- ment. In many cases that's a practical need – they cannot afford the labour (even below minimum rates) of another person. And in others, it's because the younger generation don't want to take over and can't bring themselves to have a conversation about what happens next.

Women are also coming into the profession, both as holders and as managers, but what the figures conceal is a silent force, an often unacknowledged group hidden between the lines. Generation after generation of women have been there on farms doing the paperwork, the children, and often the heavy lifting as well. They may not appear in that paperwork – and even now the course of succession often runs straight past them – but they're there. As farms begin to pass from father to daughter or from husband to widow, some are rising up out of the shadows and into the figures: 5,000 fewer men in 2012, 6,000 more women. Of the 2,500 full-time students studying agriculture at Harper Adams University in Shropshire, two-thirds are now female. Without their input – and, often, their income – those farms would now be holiday lets.

Even so, there is probably no other sector in Britain, from the oil rigs of the North Sea to the codebreakers of GCHQ, which remains as bullishly patriarchal as farming. To many, the concept that a farm could be run as well or better by a woman than a man remains as alien as it might have been to the Georgians. And it can occasionally be the women themselves who say that farms work better when they're passed down the generations to one clear successor rather than a group of siblings together. There are always reasons offered for passing away from the girl: farming requires the name to remain down the generations, farming is best done as an old-fashioned partnership with the man in the fields and the woman in the house, it's just easier if it goes to the oldest boy, women are too soft-hearted, women aren't physically resilient enough, women are great at dealing with the administrative stuff, it's too dirty, it's too depressing, it's too poor. As is often pointed out, even in an age of technology much of farming remains hard, dirty and relentlessly physical work, though it's curious that no one seems to have a problem with this in the rest of the world. Internationally, women are responsible for about two-thirds of food production, sowing, reaping, haymaking, irrigating, weeding and tending. All of which is hard, dirty and relentlessly physical. Even within the EU women hold only 12 per cent of the land but do 35 per cent of the physical labour.

And of course things are more subtle than any swingeing criticisms might imply. As those succession meetings had illustrated, where a family does still insist on primogeniture and the son (sometimes even the male cousin) does inherit, is he really better off? True, he takes the assets, the pride, the land, the house and the future with him. But in many cases he also takes the responsibility, the debts, the expectations and the critical gaze of all his neighbours. What if he doesn't want to farm? What if his sister, who has no expectations weighing on her, considers herself not discriminated against, but free?

'So,' says Heather now, looking over at the group at the furthest table: father, mother, daughter. 'It's been six months. Any changes?'

The woman – late fifties, churned-up blonde hair – glances at the daughter. 'We've talked,' she says. 'I'm not saying we got anywhere, but we talked.'

The father says nothing. His arms are folded across his chest and the line of his body makes a diagonal tipped away from his family. He is looking at the whiteboard behind Heather on which are written four words: *Challenges, Blockers, Achievements, Goals.*

'Any blockers?' asks Heather.

'Yes,' says the daughter. 'Dad.'

The father rubs the back of his neck. Slowly, it emerges that he had not been to the initial meeting six months ago, but his wife and daughter had found it so useful they had dragged him along to this one. Both parents come from farming backgrounds but had not inherited. Everything they have – 400 acres, a successful and diversified pig farm – they've built from scratch. They have two children, a son and the daughter here tonight. The boy has never been interested in agriculture and has moved to America, but the daughter has been wanting to take over since she was little.

The father is now mid-sixties and with every year that passes the fire in him burns lower. In theory he is pleased that his daughter wants to inherit, but it's more tangled than that. He pines a little for the son, and can't quite bring himself to talk about an inheritance plan. Every time the mother or daughter tries to have the conversation it stalls. Either he changes the subject or, if really pressed, he walks out of the room.

Heather doesn't ask him directly what the problem is. She just waits. Finally, he concedes. If he did start talking, if he finally brought himself to say to the daughter, all this will be yours, then the hidden side-door out of farming he'd always left ajar will finally vanish. As things stood he could in theory call the estate agents tomorrow, sell up and retire to a delightful pig-free twilight in the Dordogne. But if he makes the decision to hand the farm on, he also makes the decision to continue working with his daughter for as long as he is able. The Dordogne – and with it, his last imaginings of a life after farming – recedes.

But, says the daughter, she's done the agricultural degree, she's done the time elsewhere, she's got a plan.

'She's ready,' says Heather.

The father doesn't speak.

'We've tried,' says the mother. 'Really.' She's looking at Heather, not at her husband. 'Just a week,' she says finally, turning to him. 'Please. We need a holiday. I need a holiday.'

At the word 'holiday', the father looks momentarily deranged.

Heather passes on. The next is a man on his own. He is tall and concave, shaped like a sickle. He has put on a tie and the cuffs of his shirt are showing a careful inch from under his jacket. When he speaks his voice is full of rust. His challenge, he says, is … his challenge is … the thing is, it's not a single challenge. He stops, starts, stops again. He doesn't know where or how to describe it.

Heather coaxes out details: does anyone run the farm with him? Yes, he says. And then, no. Not really. His father is now in his eighties and has dementia, but because he refuses to see a doctor there is no diagnosis. The son has been unable to get Power of Attorney, and thus the father is still theoretically involved in all decisions. His mother died ten years ago and his sister – who now lives in Ireland – is an executor of her will but disagrees with him about the severity of the father's condition. When his mother was alive his parents ran the farm together, but his father is now querulous and embattled, fearful of being moved to a retirement home and prone to striking out. The son is now not only running the farm single-handed but also providing most of the care for his father. Somebody comes to help him a couple of days a week, but he does all the rest. He has never married, has no children, and is himself in his early sixties. He had a partner once but his parents, he says carefully, 'didn't always see eye to eye with her'. Even with a temporary improvement in lamb prices the farm is losing money. He cannot afford to employ anyone else, which means he's looking at a future caring for his father and a finite farm. He knows that the neighbouring farmer has long coveted their land.

The rest of the room is listening with a kind of livid horror. The life he is describing is one which could so easily belong to them.

Heather thanks the man, but doesn't say anything more. She looks round the room, inviting.

A woman at the next table turns in her chair. 'What do you want?' she asks.

A look of anguish passes across the man's face. Whatever he first thinks, he can't say. Instead, he says, 'I don't know.'

Heather nods, thanks him, passes on to the next table. The man looks both relieved to have the spotlight taken off him, and a little punctured. It has cost him something to say all this, and he is not finished yet.

A couple in their early thirties, with the staggered look of new parents. Both are the only people in the hall wearing office clothes – she in a suit and white blouse, he in shirt and tie. By the tea urn earlier he stood as though someone had planted him. Now he and his wife are beside one another, leaning forward, arms folded. After the First World War his grandparents bought a 300-acre farm in the Cotswolds. They had a son and a daughter, and when they died they left the stock, the farmhouse and 50 acres to the son and 250 acres of prime arable to the daughter. The daughter then married a neighbouring farmer, and now the son's land and the farmhouse sits alone, a lonely island in his sister's great wheat-field sea. The sister and her family have worked hard and got richer, the brother has worked hard and got poorer: the farmhouse is probably the only home in the Cotswolds which still has an outdoor toilet. The two siblings stopped speaking some time in the 1960s. If something needs to get said, it gets said through solicitors at £100 a keystroke. The son's son – the one speaking – has only ever seen his aunt and his father in the same room twice in his life, and one of those times his father walked out. Though he very much wants to farm, he and his father do not get on. He left the farm fifteen years ago and now has a career in aeronautics and a young son who doesn't even know he has a grandfather. His father is broke, in debt, too proud to sell, and wants to fund his own retirement by renting the farm out. If he's forced to sell, the son expects him to offer the farm to anyone but him.

While he recounts all this – neutral, distant, like somebody reading from a notice – his wife stares into the curtains. As her husband speaks, a faint blotching rises beneath her collar.

'What's your take on all this?' asks Heather.

'Maybe better if I don't say,' says the wife.

'Do you want to farm?'

'Yes,' she says.

'Do you want to farm there?'

'Yes.'

'Do you want to farm?' Heather asks the man.

'Yes.'

'Do you want to farm there?'

'No,' he says.

Once each person has had a chance to have their say Heather summarises the obstacles. Then she offers up a few apparently random thoughts: what do the other siblings want, is inheritance really the only option, what does the farm represent? The mood is charged, the room full of unspent words.

There's a break for dinner. Lamb stew, mashed potatoes. The different families break up a little. As they stand by the table spooning meat onto their plates, one farmer talks to another – something about the harvest, something about the Ministry, nothing about what's just passed. Something, some constraint in the room, has eased, but not so much that people will speak freely to each other. At the tables everyone is talking animatedly about the past summer's landmarks – weddings, Three Counties, operations. The mood is loaded, conspiratorial.

Simply to have got these people in a room with each other is an achievement. You could sit in a pub any night of the week and listen to farmers talking about farming, but there's a difference between those discussions and these. In the pub, there is no pain. There is complaint – Brexit, inflation, feed costs – but there is never any real damage done. The kids are just going through a tricky patch, the violence is always manageable and nobody mentions the flashing blue lights in the middle of the night. Everything, always, is fine. Things are a bit sticky maybe, but basically fine. The acreage is always double and the debt is always a tenth of what it really is. The only exception to that rule is epidemics: foot-and-mouth, bTB, Covid-19. But here, in this room, between these farmers, is something a bit closer to honesty.

Often Heather can find herself called to a meeting which is apparently about money but is really about something else. As GPs often note, there is the appointment (headaches, nasty cold) and then, just before the goodbye, there's the real reason: the sadness, the unidentified lump. In addition to being physically the most dangerous job in Britain – on a par with deep-sea trawling for the sheer reckless nihilism of its safety record – farm work has a reputation for doing as much damage to its workers emotionally as it does physically.

It's impossible to generalise, but farmers as a rule do not talk. They don't talk because farmers are supposed to be self-reliant, to cope, to be resilient in the face of triumph or disaster. If your spouse is your partner not just in marriage but in business, if they are parent to your children and also your lawyer, secretary, financial adviser, nurse, strategist, mechanic and secondary income stream, if you know that any mention of the words 'inheritance' or 'future' is followed by an explosion, then why would you talk? The stakes are far too high. In the past decade borrowing has doubled, but fewer than half of farmers are making a living. If you have to have a talk about handing the farm to one child over another or about selling land, and every time you've tried to have those conversations before it's led to a month of silence, then why would you try again? Why wouldn't you, sometimes, feel that there was no future other than a worse one? As another succession facilitator, Siân Bushell, puts it, 'Depression is about shame for everybody, but more so for farmers, because they have this facade and they're very self-reliant people, so to be depressed is shameful for them. They'd rather throw a rope over a beam and hang themselves.'

In situations where she feels out of her depth, Siân, like Heather, will get other individuals or agencies involved. Particularly in cases where there might be drink or drugs involved, or if there's a clear threat of violence. Stimulants – or depressants – are nothing new to agriculture. Alcohol and farming have gone together for as long as grain has fermented, and if the world is generally less agitated by the thought of a farmer with a drink problem than a farmer with a drug problem, that's only because the results of drinking too much while using heavy machinery are better known. As with other endurance events there is always the temptation – the need, almost – to ease yourself up to a point where spending several weeks driving very slowly up and down fields watching ripe barley fall everlastingly beneath your blades seems like a reasonable, or even an attainable, pursuit. As farming has grown bigger, so there's just more of things – more potatoes, more apple trees, more rapeseed or maize. More lines. And all of it has to be planted or harvested at exactly the same moment. And, unlike other occupations, farming has no compulsory dope tests.

Heather goes to the front again, issuing instructions. The room changes and the tables are reassembled into three groups. Each table is presented with an imaginary scenario: a failing farm near a large town, two brothers, two more off-farm siblings who want their money out of the business, a dairy partnership which either expands or dies, potential residential planning permission on some of the land. Each individual role-plays one of the characters (sibling, partner, daughter-in-law). After half an hour the whole group has to come to a conclusion about the farm's future. By exploring the business from the point of view of one imaginary individual, each person has an opportunity to see his or her own situation from a different perspective. An ageing male farm manager takes the position of a twenty-something daughter with a family of her own and no interest in farming. A grandmother has to take the part of a grandson who wants to buy all his siblings out and be left to farm with his husband. Her lips pucker with the effort.

Afterwards, each group's solution is explained to the room: invest and expand, involve the off-farm siblings, get out of dairying, try something else instead. Not one person from any of the groups suggests selling the farm, or the land.

Part of the reason it can be so difficult to walk away is because farming offers a complete way of being. It isn't just a job, it's an inheritance – an identity. Which then makes it difficult for the children to say, I want to study law or get a job in Mozambique, because that might sound like a rejection not just of farming but of their upbringing too. Which means in turn that the place drags along its own unbrakeable logic. For those who don't want the weight of that legacy, who has the strength to sell? Who wants to be the one to disappoint the Dead Ones? Who wants to be the one who finally says, no, enough? Stop?

Gradually, through all the talk of diversification, of succession and post-Brexit changes, a shape from beneath begins to break surface. By getting all these people here, by letting them speak of private matters in a public space, it's as if something has finally become visible which was hidden before.

Over and over every one of the families talks about The Farm as a fourth presence, a character in its own right, a personality larger and more dominant than any single individual. Their farm has its own needs and drives, its own determination, its own ecosystem of luck, faith and judgement. It doesn't matter if they are owners or tenants, what acreage they have or what type: every person here treats the farm and the land as a living thing. Even in a village hall, each person here has brought their buildings and fields along with them. They wear the farm in their clothes. They wear it in their aches and pains, their mended bones, the movements they repeat every day. It's marked on their faces and in the way they stand, it's branded on their hands and in the shape the lines take in their skin. It was the farm that came swaggering in here first, the farm which squats over these proceedings, the farm which explains them or dictates to them.

For some that farm's personality is tyrannical, capricious, a jealous god separating and enslaving. Scattered among the families are a few individuals who either talk very little, or – when they do talk – use the same language they might use in a marriage long gone rotten. They are exhausted, used-up, discouraged, and there's something monstrous in the way they describe the place: the autocracy of its demands, the spite of bad weather or broken machinery, the energy they give it and the debts they owe, the hole in the money getting bigger and bigger until the fear of money's absence is all they can see any more. The way they describe their lives – the sacrifices, the vanished years, the drink and broken things, the fissures drifting wide between one side of the family and another, the great green darkness clouding everything else out of sight – has a weight heavier than the land itself. It comes from a tiredness gone far beyond resentment. They might – they do – resent each other, but the farm itself is just a fact like twenty-four hours is a fact. For them the rotation of the seasons is a millwheel grinding on, the transition from one generation to another is the shifting of a dead weight from one shoulder to another, and any talk of possibilities is just a waste of dreams. The farm is forever, six generations, four-score years and ten, an ancestral life sentence.

'There's no exit strategy,' one woman says. 'The exit strategy is death.'

Sitting here watching the places written on the people, I recall something the Baptist minister Ifor Williams had said. He and his wife live in mid-Wales, and round there farmers are often named not by their first and surnames but by their land. So a man known as Gareth Lloyd is Gareth Glan-Rhiew,

Alan Richards is Alan Coed-y-Nant. Ifor had recently gone to the funeral of a local farmer known generally as David Cefn Garth, but on this occasion things had been taken one step further. On the front of the printed order of service, where a photograph of the person and their dates would normally be, there was no picture of the man. Instead there was just a cross, and an image of the farmhouse. Only the house, nothing else. The farm had eaten the farmer.

But if to some the farm is despotic, then it's equally plain that others feel differently. They understand that they have an apparently intractable problem (debt, no successors), but beneath that there is a healthy bank balance and a will to work. The majority of the younger generation here talk of the farm as a business, a set of challenges requiring certain skills, but no more than that. They are more dispassionate than the older ones, clearer about the practicalities of a life beyond subsidies, energised by visions of new things to pull out of the old ground. Farming, they say repeatedly, is a job, and the farm – their own farm – is just an opportunity with grass attached. They might have been born to it, but they don't have to die for it.

And then there's a few in whom that sense of a personality embodied in a place is just as strong, but in their case it's more benign. At the back of their voices there is still a note of love and wonder, and in their faces is the light of people who have somehow lucked out in life. Despite the eighteen-hour days, despite the caprices of supermarkets or parts suppliers, they see the same things differently – 'lovely hot summer, harvest better than expected, doing nicely with this TV location thing'. Nobody talks about being a custodian or steward of the land. Instead, they talk as if they and the land are bound in partnership, and that both parties have collaborated down the generations in a deep-reaching relationship. In their version the farm is a genius loci, an abundant god of warmth and rewards.

The soil has been kind, and goes on being kind. The weather is difficult, the market impossible, but the ground on which they rest is true. There is friction – they wouldn't be sitting here if there wasn't – but that's more to do with the differing wills of people, not the place itself. In everything they say, there is the absolute intention not just to keep going but to honour the place as much as it has honoured them.

Listening to the meaning between what they say, both good and bad, I think, people never talk this way about offices. A few months before this meeting I had heard a young farmer in Dorset describing lambing with her father. Depending on the size of the flock or the time the ewes were tupped, lambing can last for months. Every year when the season started her father would bring the stereo from the house and set it up in the shed. When she or her brothers or her dad started to get sleepy they'd listen to the radio, but mostly on the cold night watches he would look for something classical. She talked about sitting there in the straw for hours, stoned with tiredness, watching the ewes turning in the straw until their gaze reached inward and the time was right to plunge her hand into the tangle of legs, pulling the scrappy lambs into the world, knowing that she had drawn out the life inside. Just before dawn she would walk out of the shed on the hill and gaze up. In her memory it was always frosty, and the great velvet cosmos was always spread above her, and the enchanted ground always glittered. She could still feel the new lambs' warmth on her skin and the music – Mozart, Bach, Grieg – poured out of the walls and down the hill as if it was that hill and the hill itself had made it.

Her father had long ago sold the farm and she now worked in a different part of the country. But there were days when she would have given anything to be that tired and that content again.

4

Hedge Funds

If someone from a city planned a hill, this is probably what it would look like. A gentle slope with a combover of bracken rising up to a slabby summit and a trig point pinned to the top like the pivot on a compass. From a distance there's a few sheep-shaped splodges and a scattering of trees with their underleaves razored off to grazing height. Close up, the grass and bracken give way to heath and heather. Up here all the plants have gone horizontal, lying low to the ground and creeping against the wind. From a place of comfort it becomes a place where everything has been laid flat by the sheer ordinariness of bad weather. You need to retrain your habits of looking in order to scale down and see detail, subtlety, tiny thriving life. And then you get to the top of the hill and suddenly there is a land so splendidly green it seems bewildering, a place where the fields and the spaces between fields have been worked over for so long they've taken on the discreet radiance that only very well-used things get. It's a landscape overstitched with hedge lines and seamed with rivers, a place that looks cared for and abundant. And then on the other side there are the towns, angular in winter, grey lines blowing like ash over the valleys.

The upper part of the hill has always been common land, meaning that a small number of people have the right to keep animals here. Often, those rights cover only the grazing of sheep, but they can include other forms of stock (pigs, cows, ponies) or offer legal gleanings from the days before the land was enclosed (rights in the soil, rights of animals *ferae naturae*, rights of pasturage, estover, pannage, turbary or piscary). Though in theory commoners' rights also allowed them to take firewood or to shoot wild animals, those rights were only inter- mittently asserted. These days most of the commoners worked in the city, and considered the rights irrelevant throwbacks to a time when men wore smocks. Those farmers who did have animals on the hill sometimes came into conflict with the new locals, who valued the common mainly as a place to get more than two bars of signal on their phone and didn't see why a piece of land belonging to everyone didn't also belong to span- iels off the lead. Bert wasn't much interested in the common. He'd never gone for a non-working walk in his life and, though he liked the space it gave, he definitely preferred the kind of land which could be owned.

Until the foot-and-mouth crisis of 2001 Rise had always been a mixed farm – mainly beef cattle and sheep, but also turkeys, chickens (for the eggs), geese, the horses, and three Jersey cows who donated their milk in return for giving all the children a good kicking once in a while. Bert and his sisters were expected to milk the cows by hand before school in the morning and after returning in the evening, and though Bert was good at rugby, Gerwyn's insistence on his son's attendance meant that from the age of sixteen Bert never spent a night away from the farm. In the end he only did so because he developed appendicitis aged twenty-five and had to be taken to hospital.

What was striking was Rise's self-sufficiency. Or perhaps, what was striking was how far, in the space of a century, the rest of the country had wandered from that sufficiency. For many millennia farming's evolution was so closely bound to subsistence that they were one and the same. You grew the food you needed to eat to stay alive, and then you grew the food you needed to sell to others for them to stay alive. The point of a farm or a smallholding was to produce enough to feed a household, a village or a county. If the Howells had geese, then the Craddocks at Little Acre down the lane would have ducks or Shire horses or a mill, and the farm beyond them might do a bit of weaving or coopering on the side, and somehow all the necessary jobs in the district would get done. The whole arrangement at Rise was the product of a farming system which had turned from a state of life or death to something which, even by the Millennium, was only a little more industrialised. It also represented a tested way of hedging bets. If the price of one stock fell, then another should take up the shortfall. If turkeys didn't have a good Christmas, then surely venison would. If liveweight prices for beef cattle were down, then bacon might save the day. Prices were always volatile long before the global marketplace came along, and it always made sense for any farmer not to put all his eggs in one basket.

Even so, the calculation about what to keep, and how, and why, was also moved by less rational forces than mere money. Bert hadn't just kept pigs because they were a valuable form of income: he kept them because he was a good pig man. He was fond of them. He enjoyed looking after them, enjoyed their personalities and habits, liked breeding betterness in them. He also savoured his local reputation as a man of quality who knew how to draw out the best, and the general understanding that anyone who bought one of his sows was getting a true standard. Bert was a fair dairy farmer and a competent keeper of poultry, but his best stockmanship was always reserved for the pigs. Livestock farmers were often one thing but not the other – had a knack with cows but were not so good with sheep, stood no nonsense from the hardest bull but couldn't get the hang of hens.

And these lands did breed excellent stockmen. The Welsh borderlands have rarely been rich – too hilly – so they were never subject to the booms and busts of richer counties. Like the Lake District or the Highlands, they could grow trees but not huge acreages of arable crops so unlike East Anglia or Oxfordshire, this was not a place known for wheat or barley. The county archive holds the censuses going back to 1841 and, until well into the twentieth century, each one lists the majority of the rural population as either 'ag lab' (agricultural labourers) or paupers. Rural Britain was itself split into towns, large country estates, farms (often no more than a couple of dozen acres) and smallholdings. On the old field plans each one has an area of garden and pasture, a field for growing crops or hay and – if they were relatively prosperous – somewhere for keeping the cows or a horse.

Despite regular agricultural depressions and the dispersal of many grand estates, the broader land is often still explained by the Big House and its encirclement of tenant farms. Along the valley there's the river, the blanket-stitch line of the railway and a smirr of woodland fallen to one or other War. For all the changes – grain silos, telegraph poles, new housing developments – it is the trees which still shape the landscape in most parts of Britain. In areas where large-scale commercial forestry predominates, blocky slabs of conifer lie flat on the hillsides, slapped on like paint. In other parts of the country rows of poplars have been planted as windbreaks or privacy screens, cutting out the borders of fields or surrounding the roadsides. Farmers often have a reputation for disliking trees – get in the way, not enough value, awkward to plough round – but in reality trees were as essential to the life of a farm as fields were. In summer they cast shade for the stock, in winter they held water, in youth they provided fruit and in age they were felled to become future farm buildings. They are the strainer posts and telegraph poles, the ceilings and the floors, the fodder and the heat, the record of the past and the marker for the future. In almost every conflict the forests come down, turned into anything from trebuchets to pit-props, and the crops go up. The land changes again, shifts, readjusts, regrows over and over to provide a living for more people: harder use, abandonment, reinstatement. During the twentieth century the flatlands in the haunch of Eastern England had everything superfluous to food removed from the landscape by the mid-1940s. Trees and hedges were grubbed up, roads were straightened and rivers unwriggled. The fields doubled in size and then doubled again. Dairy cattle became capable of producing seven times the amount of milk a calf would need, sheep were suddenly so beefy that when they lay down they couldn't always stand upright again. The victors might have won, but they just kept on digging.

But while the acreage of productive agricultural land increased, the numbers of people working it plummeted. By the early twentieth century when Ron Gifford was being marched to work by his father the agricultural workforce had already declined to a million. It fell further during the 1920s, rose temporarily during the war, and dwindled throughout the remainder of the twentieth century. Now, two decades into the twenty-first, it stands at a skeletal 180,000.

David's generation of farmers have always belonged to a landscape in which farms either survived by growing fat or getting thin. In Bert's day a farm of 180 acres could, if well-run, have kept a family of six or seven, plus perhaps another full-time worker and maybe some seasonal help. By the 1990s the economics had twisted and narrowed. Competition between cooperatives and supermarket buyers had driven prices down to a point where farming was only viable with the subsidy or by shedding the extra labour. Hence the farms run by an

73

older couple drawing no wage for their work or where the real income is derived from diversification. The tracks of farming might still score the countryside, but the farmers themselves seemed to have disappeared. The big collective moments in the agricultural calendar – hay-making, shearing, gathering – had become incidental. Units of village time were measured in Christmases, half-terms and quiz nights rather than round-ups and harvest suppers. Farming had gone to ground.

After the 2001 outbreak of foot-and-mouth Bert and Alison restocked with sheep alone. Though Rise is a hill farm, they chose Welsh Mules from Bluefaced Leicester tups and Welsh Mountain ewes, which gave them the Bluefaces' productivity combined with the Mountains' resilience and good mothering qualities. To many people, a sheep is a sheep – a white woolly thing about so high, eats grass, international shorthand for sameness. But to a sheep farmer, the difference in temperament, value and productivity between one breed and another would be as profound as the difference between a chihuahua and a wolfhound. Some farmers focus on one or other characteristic, breeding for the best lean meat or the easiest temperament or a sheep which looks spectacular in the showring. Most breed for a combination of qualities: prolific lamber but hardy, grows fast but low-maintenance. Good parenting qualities are particularly important. According to Bert, Welsh Mules (distinguishable by their long ears and freckled faces) have lower rates of teenage pregnancy than other breeds. Teen ewes (a year old) can sometimes abandon their lambs and often need considerable persuasion to return to motherhood. Upland sheep (Blackfaces, Welsh Mountains, Cheviots, Herdwicks, etc.) tend to be smaller, leggier, more resilient. They can be fine-featured and agile and will probably stay out on the hills all year. They lamb themselves, are good mothers, and are often hefted – i.e., they belong to one patch of land and will not stray from it. The lowland breeds (Texels, Lleyns, Bluefaced Leicesters, Suffolks) are generally larger and are prolific lambers, meaning that most pregnancies result in twins or triplets. They tend to be lambed inside and – even with cross-breeding for resilience – may be less hardy than mountain breeds. They're the ancestral results of generations of meat-breeding, full of corners and angles, efficient and brute-faced. A four-horned Hebridean might look alarming, but being charged by a Texel would be like being rammed by a reception desk.

Every autumn the sheep at Rise Farm would be scanned and marked accordingly – a blue splodge for triplets, green for barren, orange for twins. All of them have already been marked with a dark red H for Howell, a yellow or orange blur to show the precise week they were tupped (and thus the week they will lamb), and pink for any sheep requiring separate medication.

All those different colours are a reminder of what it takes to raise some of the more high-maintenance breeds to the point of sale. By 2002, when the domestic and the export market had recovered sufficiently from the effect of both the BSE and foot-and-mouth disease outbreaks, a three-year-old ewe might reach £90 at market. Fifteen years later it would be lucky to get within sight of that price. Which, considering that the Howells had birthed it, fed it, nursed it, watered it, tagged it, pulled it seven times out of whichever hedge/fence/gate/ditch it had got itself into, paid the vet's fees, sheared it, foddered it, fed it, tupped it, transported it, wormed it, drenched it, dipped it, scanned it, passported it, lambed it, lambed it again, taken it 20 miles to the nearest market, haggled over the liveweight price and had it safely, traceably and legally sold to an abattoir supplier, some-times didn't leave change from treble again. As for the fleece, only certain breeds yield saleable wool – the rest usually only just covers the cost of shearing. Even with the subsidy it would be tricky to argue that sheep farming was easy money.

So farming requires a certain resilience. Do you hold off going to market until prices rise, even if that means you've got 300 lambs in a shed all eating their heads off? Do you stake the farm on the price today when it might be higher tomorrow? Do you believe that goats are the future, or should you try going all out for biomass? How many sleepless nights will you trade in exchange for a new dairy unit, and exactly how much debt is too much? How do you arrange for the future when even just one element of that future – the weather – remains so magisterially unpredictable that you have no idea whether you're preparing for a flood, a drought, a hurricane or a plague? Small wonder that, like sailors, farmers can sometimes be superstitious.

This patch of ancient green is a trading floor, a gambling den, a form of spread-betting so old it gave betting its names. The terms hedging and stocks migrated from the country market to the city. A stock is still a piece of wood or a box where you keep your money, and to hedge a risk is to fence it around, to give it clear borders. A market was once always a physical space where people stood around examining actual things – tools, sheep, horseflesh. Over the decades that market began to split, one half staying in place and the other quietly removing itself from the mud and the minings, slipping further and further away until it came to rest in a glassed-out London office block where the stocks on the screens had lost all contact with the animate world and become something entirely conceptual – junk bonds, short-selling, securities. Farming remained the same: still went to market, still took risks, still leveraged the land on the rainfall next year. And still had to look their entirely animate stock in the eye first thing every morning. These are all commodities which have to be reaped before they can be sold or loaded protesting into a trailer or raised as orphans when their mother abandons them. The City may console itself by dealing in intangibles, but farmers cannot help but trade in very tangibles. They hedge on lives, on 500 kilos-worth of breathing, ruminative evolution, or on millions and millions of stalks through which the light has risen and the sap has shot. No farmer does anything but gamble on a daily round of futures. This isn't *a* market, this is *the* original market, the market from which all others came.

And though the City and the farm have ostensibly gone their separate ways – one in stripes, the other in checks – they are still bound to, and by, each other. The global price for soy affects them both. The borders have got wider but the mindset is just the same, and farming, if anything, requires a long-view coolness greater than anything practised by high-rise Masters of the Universe. In the summer of 2018 domestic lamb prices doubled and then halved within a six-week period, and there's nothing that brings the whims of a modern economy home quite like a shedful of sheep which just lost most of their value. Any sectors which are not eligible for subsidy – geese, pigs, arable, poultry – have had to get very big and efficient, or, financially speaking, they died. Understandably, one of the misconceptions about agricultural subsidies is that they are paid universally to all types of agriculture. In fact, the number of areas not covered by them is larger than those that are.

And farming is so fixed, and so everlastingly precarious. A twenty-minute hailstorm could wipe out a year's profit. One nearby farm lost eighty lambs and thus all of that year's profit in a two-hour snowstorm which didn't touch the neighbouring village. And every year, there's a kind of attrition that takes place. A farmer can do all in his power to weigh the odds, study the form and play the market, but one single variable can still make a mockery of it all: a food scare, a long winter, a bitter frost, a falling price.

*

It's 7 a.m. on a Wednesday morning in early September, and in Hereford Livestock Market a queue of identical trailers pulled by identical Mitsubishi L200 pick-ups all dented in identical places are waiting at the gate. Once through, they back up to the bays below the different signs: 'Cull Ewes', 'Store & Breeding Sheep', 'Pigs'. A larger trailer manoeuvres into place near the end of the shed. As the men open the back and let the first lambs run down towards the pens the ones above stare out from the slits in the sides, taking in the broad expanse of concrete and the scent of diesel. Below them three big men with the rounded bulk of rugby players wade up to their thighs in a milky froth of moving wool.

From out of the front seat a black-and-brown collie/terrier cross appears. His ears are set to vertical and his tail is going like a windscreen wiper. He races up the ramp into the back of the trailer, barking the last reluctant lambs down the slope. The lambs are confused, lost in unfamiliar shadows. Some have turned round and are trying to go back towards the trailer, clotting the route down the passageway. Seeing the confusion, the dog hurls himself from the back of the ramp straight onto the lambs' backs, stepping on anything – a head, an ear, a neck – so he can get over them and reach the front. Some of the lambs rear up, panicked, but the dog adjusts mid-stride, flying over a magic woollen carpet to his place at the front. The three men stand redundant in the wake of the white tide as the dog – now absolutely in command – bosses the lambs around the corner and down the corridor.

Within half an hour the whole shed is full of sheep: store lambs, prime lambs, light, medium or heavy, cull ewes and pedigrees, 3,000 of them in one section, 5,000 in another, a great wide concrete field. Despite the numbers, the majority are from just a handful of breeds: Beltexes, Texels, Suffolks, Cheviots, Leicesters, Welsh Mules, Blackfaces.

By 9 a.m. there must be 14,000 sheep in here but, apart from the call of a calf from the adjoining section and the low murmur of chat between the farmers themselves, there's very little noise. The light falls long into the shed from the east, silhouetting the men in their tired shirts. Beside them the lambs stand in the pens until the valuer comes round and sprays a red letter A or B on their backs to show their separate lots. The auction-eers move from pen to pen gripping the lambs' backs between one assessing hand to feel their condition before moving them onto the scales. Most farmers will have kept back their best for breeding or for later sale, so the majority of sheep in here are probably mid-range: the ones who have reached a reasonable target weight but are neither runts nor show-stoppers. They'll have been tidied up, ear tags all in order, no signs of disease or lameness, not showing too much effort but not none at all.

Breeding tups and cull ewes will have been kept back for separate sales, and farmers with only a handful ready can find their own markets, slaughtering at one of the smaller abattoirs and selling to local butchers. Each pen here therefore contains only new season lambs all averaged out by weight. Last night David weighed the seventeen Rise Farm lambs at an average of 48 kg each. This morning, the market valuer puts them at 44 kg. The discrepancy is not unusual. Stress, a night's rest and dehydration will make a difference, and farmers have been ques-tioning the balance of market scales since markets began. From David's point of view, the trouble is that the difference between the two weights moves those sheep from the medium-to-heavy bracket into the medium. It's not great: prices for heavy lambs are good, prices for small and medium-weights are not. A fort-night ago all prices were down. Last week, they were lower. Still, it could be worse – beef is through the floor.

Hereford is one of the largest markets in the west. Many Welsh farmers bring their animals the extra distance over the

79

border: while their local markets may be closer, the prices fetched here are often better and if there's the possibility of making £10 more per lamb many farmers choose to add the extra mileage. There's a larger pool of buyers and – if they themselves are keen on purchasing – a wider selection of stock from which to pick.

Each market also has its own identity. If you were in the south but wanted a Shetland tup, for instance, then you might take the trouble to head all the way to Dingwall in the Highlands instead of the lesser distance to Carlisle. Likewise, each market is held on a different day of the week and is subject to its own local variations, so while prices might be down on a Tuesday in Sedgemoor they could be up by Thursday in Carmarthen. Hereford's main auction is on a Wednesday, selling sheep and cattle and, less frequently, goats and pigs. Sometimes the sheep are in lamb, sometimes they are lambs. Sometimes they're breeding tups, other times they're hoggs (lambs up to about eighteen months old). Some are being sold from farmer to farmer as stores: lambs born and raised on hill farms which go to lowland farms over winter to fatten up. Sometimes the cattle on offer are pedigree offerings from a single breed, sometimes they're bulls of various breeds. Sometimes they're red or orange markets, auctions in which only cattle from herds under a TB restriction are sold. Sometimes the animals are shown and sold from the pens, and sometimes through the ring, the traditional raked circle surrounding a large enclosure with an auctioneer's stand at one end. But every time, the point is to sell.

The loudspeaker announces the start of the auction in fifteen minutes. A small grouping of farmers has already started to cluster around the far pens, shifting around to get a better view or pacing the rows to inspect the goods on offer. When they stop and lean over the bars, it is their hands which suddenly seem most conspicuous, lumpy and stubbed, or with one or other finger joint awry and so striated with veins they look like something dug from the ground. Some are crooked with arthritis, others bloated with alcohol, but all are definite records of who their owners are, what they've done and how long they've been doing it for. The women's hands are thin and stiff, the sort of hands you get from a lifetime of rehanging cold gates or grabbing at the nearest handful of passing sheep, the wedding rings now locked on under knuckles burred by overuse.

The auctioneer (a brickish, bent-backed figure in water-proof chaps) climbs up onto a walkway between the pens, and without preamble begins muttering into a headset, a clerk beside him noting the figures. The rhythm of his speech seems private but impersonal, a practised inflectionless patois. Every livestock auctioneer has his own particular poetry, a sing-song rap in three-four time conducted over the backs of the beings being sold. Some auctioneers manage a flat mathematical plain-chant broken occasionally with rears in volume or scale – 'two HUNdred, two one, two two, two HUNdred and TWENty guineas' – and some almost break into song – 'WUNfiveeight, WUNfiveEIGHT, WUNfivenine, onefivenine, onesixtyoneSIX-TYonesixty AND aaat WUN-six-WUN' – but the pace here is more conversational, a deal made in front of spectators but designed only for buyers. The auctioneer gestures over the rail down at the sheep, moving slowly down the rows followed by his attentive flock.

Leaning over the pens directly opposite the auctioneer are three men, tall, middling and small. All of them are late fifties, red-faced and wattle-necked, shirts open to the third button. They've all got a phone in one pocket and a pair of reading glasses in another, and as each lot sells they scribble the price on the backs of paper catalogues or calculate the odds of an easy deal. Occasionally they exchange a word with the clerk or query a mishearing, but otherwise they do not acknowledge either each other or any of the people clustered round them.

The three men are the buyers for the big abattoirs around Wales and the West Midlands. These men buy the stock on behalf of their clients, and then the supermarkets and the exporters buy from them. By the time the market ends today, they will have bought the majority of the lambs in this shed. Within a couple of days those lambs will have been taken to their respective places of slaughter and killed, moving as they leave this world from a liveweight price to a deadweight one. A few penfuls will have been bought by one of the three men for overwintering at his own farm, while many of the older sheep will be sold to buyers for halal abattoirs and butchers. Most will go for export: France, Germany, Belgium. Over the past few decades the British have been gradually losing their appetite for lamb, replacing it either with other red meats or chicken, or abandoning it entirely for more herbivorous options. Currently, it is only Muslim consumers who are sustaining the market anywhere near previous levels. Halal buyers now account for a fifth of the total UK trade in lamb. Ewes whose value was once considered spent after three or four pregnancies continue to sell for decent money, and the annual lamb slaughter for Eid, the festival of the breaking of the fast at the end of Ramadan, now always causes a welcome spike in prices.

The farmers watch the auctioneer, one arm propped on the bars. As each lot is sold a few turn to their neighbour and murmur something under their breath, but to the surrounding audience they seem neither happy nor sad and only the slight drop of a shoulder gives any indication that the sale meant any-thing at all. David's pen of seventeen lambs goes for £66.50 per animal. It's not the price he was hoping for. Those with heavy lambs have sold well – a farmer on the other side of the county with forty averaged at 52 kg gets £81 for each – but medium or small lamb prices are down however good the condition.

By mid-morning the work is done. The pens have emptied, the trailers are moving and in the canteen everyone is reviewing the day's proceedings over beans on toast. Outside the windows the trees spring in the breeze, but in here the clientele remains enfolded in the same torpid fug as a ferry during a hard crossing. This is a place for a pause, a respite where the rain and the wind's blows pull back for a moment. It's only 11 a.m., but everyone in here has been up since 4 or 5 a.m. and has been looking forward to the chance to eat and think – or not to think – about the way things have gone. The tables are full: old men, old women, young men, muscular, slap-faced, white-haired, tall, small, barely out of school. All white, mostly male. They've taken off their baseball caps and jackets, laid their mobiles upended on the table and are getting down to the other essential business of the day: the exchange of critical market intel.

It's easy to look at the faces in here or round the ring and see only something unchanging, a homogenous group of people who may have their disputes but whose grandfathers probably fought in the same regiments for the same dreams. But it's equally possible to look at the same group of people and see the tension writ through them between inner and outer worlds, and the pull between tradition and change. In the queue for food there are people who can't stand each other, farmers who would never knowingly exchange a civil word with the man behind them, smallholders who have been coming here since they were children, hobby farmers for whom this is all still a novelty. There are buyers, NFU reps, hauliers and, when business is done for the day, the auctioneers themselves. There are people nursing the pain of a bad sale, those sizing up the chance of private deals, those whose minds are all on the future or completely in the past. All of them exchange a word with the ladies behind the counter, and all of them get served with the sort of menu mostly coloured brown.

Outside the windows all those L200s and Discoverys, each coupled to its own empty trailer, rattle their way out of the car park towards home. The lambs have gone one way, the farmers the other. Their business with each other – birth to summer, summer to market – is at an end.

5

Cleavers

Fyle & Sons has been the village butchers in Little Barton for many decades, and has thrived for that long by doing what it does very, very well. It's consistently adored by many of the big restaurants, loved by foodies, has queues of chefs and cooks worshipping at the feet of the chill cabinets. It's a five-star village butcher, the sort of place which makes people exclaim that this – this rosy-pink vision, this thriving high-street exemplar – is what it, Britain, the countryside, should all be like. As well as supplying several big restaurants it does the local music festival and two nearby Michelin stars.

If you walk in off the street, the first person you encounter will almost certainly be a Fyle. Michael, the patriarch of the family, is seventy-nine, and his wife Sandra runs the adjoining deli, added a few years ago to provide a clean division between cooked meat and raw. Steve, their son, is out at the front of house with his wife Nancy. Then there's Dean, who isn't a Fyle but is also a master butcher, and provided the casting vote on whether or not to allow me to visit. There's also an apprentice, Oliver Selby – young, tall, studded with cold sores – and two part-time slaughtermen.

As customers come and go, enquiring about how to cook this or that, adding bacon or subtracting eggs, the shop hums with a steady, comfortable banter, regulars greeted by name, weekly orders already prepared. A peeling row of TripAdvisor stickers and yellow Post-Its have been pressed into the back tiles behind the butcher's block, and above it are the hooks and saws of the Fyles' trade line up on a rail. A large and well-sharpened meat cleaver waits, poised immobile just above Michael's head while he slices up a couple of steaks. There's a sense of ceremony here, an implication that, while you might have come in for something modest – half a dozen eggs, a bottle of vinegar – you will leave with an indistinct feeling of enrichment and a sense that simply by being in the shop and exchanging a few words, you've been a participant in a community with meaning and weight.

Together, the Fyles and Dean radiate a magnificent protein-fed vigour, a sense of bonhomie so conspicuous that it's easy to imagine them bursting into some kind of choral tribute to the efficacies of hard work and good meat. Michael in particular appears to have discovered some fundamental elixir of human life – though nearly eighty he's the most public face of the business, a short, solid man with a proprietorial smile and the wrists of a bricklayer. In addition to preparing meat and advising on methods of cookery, his chief role is to keep the accounts – not the finances, but the public and historical accounts of the Fyles' role in Barton and the importance of butchery in general. He is an energetic recorder of the apparently disastrous gap between Then (any time from late Bronze Age to mid-1980s) and Now (any time since DEFRA), and maintains a well-exercised set of views on everything from working practices ('Long hours in them days, had to take the meat to 'em'), foot-and-mouth ('A complete farce, it was, a farce'), the decline in village entertainment ('When I was slaughtering, kids used to come and watch'), the Food Standards Agency ('Wants doing away with. Do you know, they complained about the cat? Steve offered to buy it some wellies'), and bureaucracy ('Bloody wash forms – bloody bonkers').

Back at the turn of the new century, new regulations introduced after BSE meant that Fyles was faced with a choice: adapt, or fall. Michael launches into the story with the air of someone who has told it often and enjoys the telling of it more each time. So: he was in the slaughterhall one day when 'a little upstart with a clipboard' arrived. '"Ohhh," he said, "you can forget about this place."' The upstart took a quick look around and offered Michael a choice: spend £80,000 adapting and improving the buildings, or find another job. 'And he was a … little bugger, you know, typical, got a bit of a uniform, they love it, don't they?'

Behind him Steve rolls his eyes.

'Anyway. The chief vet, he rang me on a Monday evening at home. "Mr Fyle," he said, "I've been looking at your plans, and no way could you be able to afford this on the present number you're killing."'

Steve catches my eye and jerks his head towards the back.

'He said, "That's going to cost about £80,000." "That's about what I estimated it," I said. "Anyway," says the vet, "tell me, are you prepared to spend £20,000 to keep it? I don't mean now, I mean over three years."'

Behind him, Steve beckons.

Michael turns to serve a customer. I follow Steve past the counters through the back of the shop to the kitchen, a friendly space yellowed with the fug of old fry-ups. From the hooks on the back of the door he hands me a white coat and a hairnet. 'Trust me,' he says. 'I'm saving you from a fate worse than death. Once my father starts talking he can't stop. I don't know how many times I've heard that story.'

At the head of the table two silent figures in white coats crouch over a laptop. Beside them are two mugs of half-drunk tea and a pile of FSA forms. They look up at our arrival and then back down again.

'Right,' says Dean, appearing through the back door. 'Come with me.'

At the back of the *Farmer's Guardian* there is a series of tables giving the prices achieved at UK markets for different kinds of agricultural produce over the past seven days. The tables come after the sponsored content and before the crossword, and are split by mainland nation – England, Scotland, Wales. Livestock is first, then crops, then dairy, and then a mixed basket including the UK monthly milk prices, soya hulls and hay bales. Some items listed are seasonal (oilseed rape) and some are constant (milk, deadweight steers), and the tables can be read either by commodity (wheat) or by market area (Northallerton, Ruthin). In this nerveless form everything, animal, vegetable or mineral, flattens out into a number, a clean grey digit which could just as well represent the annual square-metre volume of new tree plantation or the monthly record of minor tax reliefs. But to anyone within the farming world the tables translate into a more shaded narrative. Hidden among the grey there are fortunes lost and found, gambles that paid off and debts that never did, love, divorce, the contraction of some markets or the expansion of others, new ventures, old habits. This is a record of the health and immunity of farming itself, an account of the rise of poultry or the fall in veal, the power of supermarkets and the stolidity of Britain's favourite vegetable, the potato. Last year lamb prices were low but stable, but this year they're up and down like a heart attack. Pig prices are steady, but a bale of hay can fetch about double the price of the ewes it feeds. Wheat is falling but sugar beet is rising, milk is high but heifers are low. There's a glut of apples but a shortage of organic barley, too much maize but not enough fodder. Somewhere across these pages you can read the fortunes of geography – north versus south, west against east – or the caprices of weather: hard spring, dry summer. It's a diary of a year in numerical form, a chronicle of stress foretold, a paper harvest pulled from a growing land. In its purest form this is, like farming, a statistical representation of sex, death and all the ground between.

And then, right at the bottom, dropped down low in a little section at the end of the stock pages, is a table which requires no translation at all. The figures are drawn from abattoirs all over the country and give the total weekly slaughterings for pigs, sheep and cattle. These are the animals killed at abattoirs around the country and then sold on to processors around the country who then sell it on to us in the form of a packet or a meal. This is the week's record of the animals we deem good enough to eat. In financial terms, these are the lucky ones.

Though of course the data itself varies, its constancy does not. The figures appear faithfully every seven days of every month in every year, come rain, shine, snow, Covid or Christmas. In this case, the numbers are not broken down by place or sub-classification but aggregated nationally: in one week in mid-May 2018, for instance, 172,680 pigs, 215,190 sheep and 356,650 cattle were slaughtered – a rise in all sectors from the same time the previous year. Given the question mark over red meat consumption, it seems surprising that the size of the national flock either remains steady or keeps increasing. The current UK human population is 67 million. The current UK sheep population is around 36 million, down from a high of 44.5 million in 1992, of which just under half will be slaughtered every year. Chickens, which are a comparatively new addition to the statistics, are registered separately.

It might be at this point that even the most assiduous carnivore might hesitate and consider the unseen and (mostly) unmourned mass killing those figures represent. They offer the raw truth of our national diet: our Saturday burgers and our lamb koftas, our midweek lasagne, our hungover fry-up and our last-minute fajita. They're the special-occasion Chinese meal or Sunday roast, the curling corners on the buffet slab or the abandoned pizza topping. They are our national protein and our monounsaturated fats, our iron and selenium, our trace elements. They are much of what is great about British cooking, but they're also the indifferent or discarded. Those figures give not just the meals – and thus the animals – that mattered to us, but all the stuff we didn't think about, the packets tipped away unopened or the two sausages eaten from the tray of eight.

The tables aren't designed to be emotive or censorious or to start an argument for or against. Quite the opposite. They're just a dispassionate abstract of the facts. But they are also a record of something that once had being, an animal that lived and, because it lived, then died.

Out in what would once have been the back garden there's a scatter of extensions and a different view. Anyone arriving with animals would usually bring the trailer in through the car park and up to the little lane towards the back. Along its side there is a row of straw-strewn pens showing signs of recent occupation, and beyond them is another low rectangular extension in which there is a series of spaces through which each animal will move and wait. Each pen contains small groups of sheep and pigs clustered together, their ears pricked or flattened, breeds from small pale-faced hill sheep to a sow the size of a sideboard.

The animals lie asleep or alert, silent, uneasy or indifferent. They do not seem fearful, just watchful. Dean moves through them, opening gates and shutting them, pushing a couple of lambs forward or changing the order in which they come through. A lamb reverses sharply as Dean makes a grab, while a couple of Beltex lambs rustle round and round their pen. The only smells here are of animals – food, manure, warm straw. Further on, the slaughterhall itself is in an outbuilding of its own back near the kitchen. There's a clean white corridor with a cold store on one side, its hooked steel candelabra swinging with freshly stamped pig carcasses. On the right there's a room where the newly slaughtered animals are eviscerated, and just beyond that are the killing pens. Each space from car park to cold store is designed to move the animals another station along the line between life and death, the aim being to give them a brief clean trip in the swift transition from animal to carcass to meat. Somewhere along this route, what was once a cow or a pig or a sheep becomes instead joints of beef or loins of pork or lambs, chopped.

As Michael had been explaining, Fyles is exceptional partly for the quality of its meat, but mainly because it's one of the few butchers left in Britain to run a small abattoir designed to supply not just its own needs but the requirements of anyone locally with a few beasts to butcher. Here at the back of the shop they're slaughtering for farmers who live a few miles away, or for smallholders who, once or twice a year, load one or two of their sows into a trailer and run them down the hill to their end.

Fyles runs the abattoir only two days a week and uses two part-time slaughtermen, Lloyd Corlett and Cayo Fazakas, who says so little during the time I'm there that I know no more than that he's small, dark and licensed to kill. Pigs and lambs will have been brought in the night before, but cattle – which have to be slaughtered and hung within an hour of arrival – are brought in according to carefully timetabled afternoon schedules. There are no cattle here today.

The slaughterhall is small, metal-lined, with wide grilles in the floor. Suspended above the sink there's a radio tuned to BBC Radio 2's lunchtime show, while the sound of intermittent banging comes from out the lid of the pig tank. The tank is a huge piece of kit, a great big lump of engineering set somewhere between a coffin and a chest freezer dominating one end of the hall and shaped like a lengthwise barrel. One after another, every freshly killed pig is laid into the tank, the lid is closed, the barrel starts rotating and water is pumped into the bed to wash off the carcass. The temperature is set hot enough to scald off the pig's bristles and clean its skin but not hot enough to start cooking it. Throughout the morning its uneven rumble makes a sound like a distant launderette, the smaller sows no more than a wallet stuck in a washing machine but the big boars sprawling over the sides like drunks on park benches, trotters drooping, one ear raised. Once every few minutes a froth of bristles and muck slops out and over the side, while a low tide-line of pink foam rises and recedes, exhaling itself down and into the grilles. When Lloyd or Cayo raises the lid, steam wreathes over the figure within. As they reattach the winch the vapour half parts and the shrouded figure is hoisted up, pink and streaming.

It's the sounds that catch first: the winch, the knife, the saw. On the end wall there is a partition covered by a plastic curtain which leads through to the killing pens with a winch running across the ceiling between the two spaces. Pulp's 'Common People' overlaps an intermittent bleating from outside: '*Everybody hates a tourist ...*'

The stop-start clank of the winch pulling the sows across, the way their flesh moves and settles, Cayo positioning each body to lie down in its watery end: there's something about their juicy pale Caucasian-ness and the five-foot-something height of the pigs when hanging from the winch that makes it difficult not to mark the distance – or lack of it – between them and us. A faint arhythmical scrape as Lloyd winches the pig by the tendons of its back legs out of the barrel and begins work on it, flaming off the last bristles with a blowtorch, cutting out the anus, flicking away the trotters. Beneath the horn the sow's feet are tiny and delicate, spots of blood making them seem for a second almost painted. I watch the pigs' ears, the millennia of ingenuity with which this body has been designed, then the long unzipping slit from breastbone to bladder and the slip of the innards out and onto the floor, the familiar shock of all that was so perfectly packed inside now gross and untidy as it falls away. The inner organs are slithery, not the same flexible texture as flesh but gleaming, as if all these parts which so completely belong to one body become alien and general as soon as they're displaced.

Beside the window there's another hoop with eight hooks, like a smaller version of the ones next door used for hanging the carcasses. Suspended from each of the hooks are the heart, lungs and liver of each pig. The lungs are pale and slightly grainy, the livers a plummy vinous red, and there's something about their winged shape as they hang there like the form of a mantling bird. I stand there between the lungs and the offal bin in my white coat, too stunned to do anything but stare.

Lloyd casts around for the knife he'd had earlier, takes the remote control out of the front pocket of his coat and pulls the winch with the pig over this end of the room. The tink of winch chains and sawing. 'We've now got a six-foot python,' says Jeremy Vine from above the sink. Knife on bone, then back to flesh. 'When it kills people through constriction, does it stun them first?'

Dean motions me over. 'Here,' he says. 'I'll zap one for you.'

A few minutes later he reappears, pointing at the partition. 'Stand there. Watch yourself on the floor.'

On the other side of the plastic curtain is a small space

divided into three: two pens on one side, a passageway on the other and an open space at the end of the top pen through which the winch passes. Next door in the slaughterhall where they're doing the evisceration there's no particular smell – just skin and water and heat, like the smell of an old boil wash. In here, it stinks, a sharp, sour hit: the ferrous scent of blood first, then shit and fear. Through the partition Jeremy Vine is talking to a python. 'We love having visitors.'

On the far wall there's a giant pair of orange tongs connected to an electricity supply with a serrated circle at each end like the earpieces on a pair of headphones. Over the radio there's the sound of a gate opening, then an uneven banging and a hard, tight struggle for restraint. The door of the pen knocks open and Dean steps in sideways, a giant sow rocking between his feet, so thunderous with muscle and flesh and kinetic potential that she makes the smallness of the space itself seem ridiculous. She is enormous, wild, wildly alive, three times as powerful as Dean himself.

Dean doesn't hesitate. He readjusts his position, shoves the sow tight into the gap between his boots, clamps the tongs over her head and presses the button. The sow goes rictus-still, seized by the current.

Dean releases and she starts to spasm. 'Just the same as a gun, see,' he calls over his shoulder. 'Right? And that's 'im.'

He ropes one of her back legs into the loop of the winch chain, pulls her up into the second of the two pens and slits her throat. Blood spills thickly into the concrete. I listen to the heaviness of it. On the other side of the plastic curtain Lloyd winches the sow up and through, spins her round and lays her down in the dehairing machine.

Jeremy Vine: 'OK. I've got a python round me. It's seriously ... you do not want one of those in your bed.' Sheryl Crow: '*All I wanna do is have some fun ...*'

A couple of minutes later Dean walks back with me to the kitchen. That sow, he says, was maybe 250 lbs and almost certainly half wild boar. In the last decade or so a thriving trade in farmed boar meat has built up, and many breeders are now crossing domestic pigs – usually Tamworths – with wild boar to produce a sow with all the intelligence and twice the muscle of pure-bred pigs. If they can put a genuinely wild wild boar to a couple of domestic sows, then so much the better. 'It's free, isn't it? You get a wild boar, you give it to a few sows, you let it go back, you don't pay nothing, do you?' The aim is partly to get more piglets per litter, but the bonus is that wild boar meat also commands premium prices. The downside is that, by definition, the boar/pig crosses are bigger, harder and much more aggressive.

As for the actual death it's the electric shock that kills, says Dean. Effectively, the tongs give the animal an immensely powerful epileptic fit. 'Just the same as a stun gun, really. Brain-dead, lifeless. Game over.'

Each animal will already have been dead half a minute or so by the time he's slit their throat and they've bled out. The majority of British abattoirs use the same method, though halal killing is done separately with an imam present. The Fyles don't think much of it. 'Lot of chicken is halal,' says Steve later. 'Lot of McDonald's halal – they got to satisfy a lot of peoples' tastes. They reckon it's instantaneous, but I don't believe that. I think there is such a thing as a nice way of doing it – well, not a nice way, at the end of the day something's giving up its life, but that's the nature of the beast.'

Back in the kitchen Ivan the Food Standards Agency vet is still working his way silently through the forms while his assistant thumbs through the completed pile. Oliver is sitting near the window, scrolling down his phone.

I don't think, I say to Dean, groping for something to say,

that I'd really understood the difference in size and weight between those different animals.

'Oh, yeah! You kill a bull, it's over half a ton.'

So for this job you need to be physically strong?

'Yeah!' he says, in an 'of course' voice. 'If you can't lift 'em, you're no good in this trade – it's not a weak man's game. All those big pigs in there' – he nods back towards the cold store – 'I'll have to move now.'

On your own?

'Yes!' Duh. 'And the beef. Two-hundred-pound sides of beef. That fridge is full of beef I moved yesterday.'

How many animals will you kill today?

'Eighty head,' says Dean. 'Whereas Hastings [the nearest large abattoir] would probably be doing six and a half thousand.'

Every week?

'No, every day of the week.'

Jesus! Seriously?

Ollie and Dean together: 'Yeah!'

Dean: 'Our beef is hung. Their beef is electrocuted in big chambers to tenderise it. So they can kill it, cool it, cut it, and then put it in the supermarkets for people to buy. That's why they can do it cheap, see?'

Six and a half *thousand*?

Lloyd comes in, extracts five sausages from the fridge, lines them up, shoves them under the grill and sits down at the table. While they're cooking he extracts a roll-up, waves it at the room, gets a nod, lights up.

Cayo comes in and buries his head in the local paper.

Ivan's assistant looks up. 'It's mechanised,' she says. 'Everything is mechanised.'

Is it better or worse than this place?

'Can't compare it,' says the assistant. 'Can't compare.'

'They are the same.' Ivan looks down at his laptop, apparently reluctant to find himself speaking. 'They killing animals. For me, they are the same.'

To reach his level, Dean is explaining, you need to be able to slaughter as well. 'Grade it, kill it, cut it up – that's a master butcher.' At thirty-three, he reckons he must be one of the youngest in the country.

So to do this job, you need fitness and strength. What else?

'Well,' says Dean, casting around. 'You either got it or you haven't.'

What's 'it'?

'Everything.' He resettles himself, legs apart. 'You know, customers, you got to be nice, haven't you? You can't come in on a Saturday morning with a hangover and old grudges.'

Lloyd sits back in his chair, one arm across his chest, the other holding the roll-up. He has taken off his hairnet but is still wearing his spattered white coat. Here in the kitchen, apart from the soft unfolding spiral of smoke and the rise of his breathing, there is nothing to him but stillness. A fine tilth of ash falls from the end and dribbles down his front.

Do you need a particular temperament?

'Well, you can't be weak in the head, can you? You can't be easily offended. You couldn't go in there being a flower, could you? You'd be flaking out! Thick-skinned, you need to be.'

So no vegetarians here?

'Yeah, we got one.' He points back in the direction of the deli. 'We're not prejudiced.'

Lloyd's eyes are almost closed. He's maybe early forties with a concentrated bulk to him, a sense beneath of a strength made and stored over many years. Next door in the slaughter-hall his movements were measured, efficient, with the economy of energy which comes from doing a careful job many times over. As he reached for the winch or the saw they appeared as if they were extensions of himself, and when at one stage he had started casting around the room for the knife he'd misplaced it was a disruption, as if he had broken the shape of some old, half-tranced rhythm. I stand in the corner asking questions, though every time I say something I feel like I'm trespassing. The FSA vets clearly feel the same. At one stage Ivan approaches and tells me tentatively I shouldn't be here.

'She's fine,' shouts Dean across the room, seeing the exchange. 'I said she could be.'

Ivan looks at me doggedly for a second and then retreats. FSA inspectors don't have the same status as ordinary large- or small-animal vets. Regulations brought in after BSE in 2001 stipulate that a vet must be present during all slaughterings to check on the welfare of each animal and ensure biosecurity measures are followed. It's a job with a high burn-out rate. Standard large-animal vet work might occasionally be frustrating, but it does at least salt rewarding moments in with the bad ones. Only the most stone-hearted individual could withstand a job that mostly consists of travelling from place to place watching beasts being killed.

How much do you think about the animals?

'Every day,' says Dean now. 'That's the most important thing. It's a living animal. I would never kill anything I didn't have to. I love – well, I love birds, pulls at my heartstrings. I could never kill anything like that. Little tiny, I love 'em. If it's suffering or it needs to be … then I kill it. Other than that, I don't want to know.'

But these animals weren't suffering. They were just always intended for meat.

'Exactly!' says Dean. 'That's what I mean. If it was suffering or being eaten, I'll kill it. But I would never kill anything that didn't need to be – I hate that, hate it with a passion.'

He looks at the clock on the wall, puts his mug down, turns. 'When we start the lambs, I'll shout you,' he calls.

Lloyd gets up. He takes the five sausages from under the grill, drops them onto his plate, squirts on a bit of ketchup and sets to work. He became a slaughterman, he says between mouthfuls, because his dad was a slaughterman and thirty years ago when he started there was plenty of work – five or six small abattoirs in the local area. Now he works here three days a week and the rest of the time he farms his own smallholding nearby. If he could he'd probably farm full-time and give up on this work, but there's not many left with the kind of skills he has.

So what's different about the work that he does?

'Me and Dean, we're totally different. Start to finish, we do everything, you know? Slaughtermen, butchers, animal welfare officer, farmer, we can do all week.'

And younger guys don't have that?

'Mmmm,' he says. A pop as he opens a can of Coke. 'Couldn't. Couldn't do it. Don't know how to kill.'

But after training?

'Yeah, but there's no training 'em – there's no places like this, man. If I was in a factory, there's one specific job.'

So in the big abattoirs every task would be separate?

'Yeah. Yeah.' He takes another mouthful. 'Here, Cayo? Think other people could do this job, like?'

Reluctantly Cayo lowers his paper. 'No. One of a kind. Specialist.'

Do younger people want to do this job?

'No,' says Lloyd. 'My son is only six, and he absolutely loves it – loves everything about farming, loves everything about killing, but I wouldn't want him to do it. It's hard work and people want it done for nothing.'

Having finished the sausages, he returns to the slaughter-hall. Ivan sits at one end of the table, head down, his face pale over the glow of the laptop screen. Ollie sits at the other, one arm across his chest, scrolling through his phone.

So what do they make of Andersons' view that animal behaviour is changing?

'It's cattle you need to look out for,' says Ollie. 'Like this one farmer, he brings his beasts here, his cows are wild as hell. He feeds them using his tractor and they don't have much human contact, so when they come here and there's all these slaughtermen trying to push them up to the kill pen, they go wild. Some weeks the noise level coming out we've had to shut all the doors just to drown the noise out.'

Is it just cattle that try?

'Well, cattle are the ones which are going to escape because of their size – they can get up over the things, and they've got the power to knock the doors off. But pigs have been known to. I've seen pigs knock the pens off their hinges – they get their snouts in under the hinges and push them off. And lambs, if you don't shut the doors properly can jump the pens.'

Dean returns, beckons. 'Lambs,' he says.

In the slaughterhall the pig tank has been put away and the first of the newly killed lambs is jerking through the partition. Madonna on the radio: 'La Isla Bonita'. Lloyd slices the skin downwards through the belly from anus to throat, peeling away the fleece like a wetsuit. He stops when he's unpeeled it about halfway and attaches the loose skin to a bolt on the floor. He stands back and then winches the body slowly across the room so the mechanical tension pulls the remaining fleece off, disrobing the animal inside. The flesh is paler underneath than the pigs', a buttermilk colour closer to yellow than pink. The muscles are clear and defined, the sheep's shape wedgy and resistant.

Once the lamb's covering is off the rest takes on a production-line familiarity: the same incisions, the same removals, the same slit downwards and sudden spilling fall – lungs, liver, intestine, bowel, heart, the same shudder of emptied flesh as the winch moves round. The sheep seem different to the pigs. Once eviscerated – dehaired, amputated, beheaded – a pig was still clearly a pig. But the removal of a lamb's fleece somehow strips it of its identity, as if their wool *was* them. Lloyd tosses a sheep's head towards the offal bucket. It hits the side and bounces off. For a moment it just lies there on the floor, staring. It looks at me and I look at it and I don't know what to know any more. Some part of me has been thinking about mortality and violence and our dubious moral claim to do this. Another part – the recording part – is trying to remember the mechanism of the tongs. And what remains is standing there in a pool of blood and bristles trying not to look shocked.

But I know I'm not here to debate the ethics of eating meat. I'm here because this room and this end is a part of farming in just the same way that the beginning is – the lambing shed, the farrowing pen, the chicken, the egg. Not every farmer in the UK has livestock but farmers, whether they're looking after wheat or apples or pigs, are all still subject to the same cyclical laws. The lambs one man fought to keep alive in the snows of March are the same ones that same man will load in the trailer to the abattoir in September. Lloyd, Cayo and Dean are all farmers themselves – Lloyd and Dean have sheep and beef, Cayo has pigs. The time they're not in here, they're in the business of keeping animals alive. That understanding – you rear it, you nurture it, you kill it – is not an equation ever easily understood by the public, but it's there and it will continue to be there for as long as some of that public remains omnivorous.

At the end of the day as I walked out past the empty pens, what really struck me about the Fyles was the same sense of defiant fulfilment as at Andersons. In Michael and Steve and Dean there had been a pragmatism, but also an awareness of the demand to justify what they did. Like the farms they often served, both Fyles and Andersons were tight third- or fourth-generation family enterprises, though that wasn't what defined them most. It was their attitude. What both seemed to be saying was that they were proud. Proud of doing a good job to a fine standard, proud to have continued and thrived, proud of their local identity, proud to show that work off to others. But they were also keenly aware that there were plenty of people who saw the world and their work differently. They were used to answering people who didn't believe that killing animals was necessary, and who saw the things they did round the back of the shop as an unsalvable injury not just to their own souls but to the collective conscience of humanity. Those who make an active protest against it might be a minority, but Fyles also knew that there were plenty of committed meat-eaters who, if they saw the killing pens or the pig tank, might abruptly revise their food order for the week. They have, they confide, had trouble with 'people who aren't who they say they are'.

A week later I am on the motorway just beyond Glasgow. Beside the road is a field which slopes down towards the hard shoulder, and in that field are a group of cows grazing. They're small and hairy – something crossed with Anguses. One little brown calf has detached himself from the rest of the group and is standing further down, watching the cars passing. His ears are pricked and his gaze follows us, all of us, approaching and receding. We're a herd passing on our way towards other herds – work, family, football practice – in our little tin boxes, encircled by the timings of our own lives. Around him the other cows graze on, indifferent to the road. But he looks interested, as if he'd like something explained to him.

What does he see? I wonder. I know what he is to us. But what are we to him?

6

Movement Restrictions

And then Bert got shingles and then a stent, and then the diabetes became harder to manage. Or rather, managing the diabetes remained the same, but the side effects from the medication he took began to have more of an impact. He'd wake at the wrong times, sleep at the wrong times, stay tired all day. Once or twice, taking sheep to market, he nearly fell asleep at the wheel. Waiting at the traffic lights in town, he nodded off, coming back to himself with a cold jolt. What, he wondered, if that had been on the dual carriageway? What if the trailer had overturned? He grew wary of driving, particularly at night. Either Alison took him now or he didn't go at all.

When he came round to the cottage it took him a long time to get out of his boots and a long time to get back in. Putting on his old green jacket seemed to have got a lot more complicated. For at least two decades that jacket had performed much the same function as a portable shed. It was (sort of) waterproof, it was (sort of) dry, and somewhere in one of the pockets was everything he might need: ear tags, lists, change, screws, a pocketknife, phone, washers, batteries, receipts, extinct planning notices, leaves, nails, pine cones, rubber bands, keys. But now the jacket and he struggled to get on. He couldn't get his arm around the back. The sleeve was never straight. The collar sagged in the wrong places, was inside out, on the floor, kept somehow not cooperating. When he took it off the wall, nails cascaded out of the pockets. It was upside down, it no longer fitted him, it let in the rain. It was a piece of clothing, but it had gone rogue. One day without thinking I picked it up as he was leaving and held it so he could get his arms in. He turned, and for a second I saw something like rage flash across his face.

The livestock market – which had always been about far more than just money – receded. For decades, Bert's irregular trips had been one of the few times he came down off the hill. The point was not just to sell sheep but to see what others sold, and how, and for what price. He could learn more about the lie of the land, the state of the grass and the health of the economy in a single glance than from a month's worth of market reports. This was the proof of it all. This was where all the private gambles either paid off, or didn't. This was where a hard spring or a losing hand finally became visible: here in the pens, shuffling morosely round their strawed beds. Breeding, conformation, a straight back, a good eye, a well-expressed set of genes. This was where Bert could see a definite measure of his own skill. Over tea in the café with men he'd known all his life he could present a problem – passporting issues, a dispute with the haulage contractor – and have it solved by his peers.

Now, beached at the farm, he wasn't here and he wasn't there. He couldn't work and he couldn't see what work others were doing. Either people came to him or he stayed uninformed. He was behind on the news. Selling the sheep shifted from being one of his dead-body subjects to something openly spoken. Most evenings he'd be asleep in front of the TV by 8.30, then wake at 3 a.m., get up, go downstairs, read a few pages of the *Racing Post*, rouse Alison, complain. One night, groping down the corridor, he fell down the stairs. A few weeks later, mending the rusting old oil tank with their neighbour Low-Output Llew, he bashed his head so hard he opened out bone. Alison tried mopping him up, but when she saw the depth of the wound she said she'd call the doctor.

'No!' shouted Bert, reporting this conversation later. 'I don't want no fucking doctor!'

His face was a mess. Two days later there was still the same raw gash beneath the blackening scab, but something had thickened. The skin around his eyes had darkened and the sockets were outlined with shadows. His eyebrows stood out hard on his skull and his cheeks had a liverish tint, little threaded veins creeping over his cheeks.

'I'm making myself scarce,' he said, appearing one Sunday morning. 'There's a busload of morons come to look at the fireplace.' The morons, it transpired, were actually American academics from Utah researching early Mormon history. Since they had been visiting the farm every year since the 1960s, Bert knew exactly who they were. Some years he was more than capable of being civil, sitting at the far corner of the sofa, noting points of interest in the stonework and making small talk on the drawbacks of having five wives. Afterwards the historians would leave happy comments online, delighted with the antique buildings and the hospitality of their farming hosts. The comments always pleased and frustrated Bert in equal measure. He liked hearing the farm praised, but the trouble with a good review was that they might come back. If they did, they might – like this year – find him scratchy and ill-founded. Once or twice he had threatened to block the offending fireplace and smoke them all back to Salt Lake City.

In the mornings he took to pottering around in the garden, an area of the farm which until then Alison had run without fuss, producing enough tomatoes, veg, potatoes and fruit to feed not only themselves but the local market and an honesty box in the yard. By 10 or 11 a.m. Bert would have stumped down the path to the polytunnel to stand there unstringing the tomato plants. She'd find him forking weakly over potting compost or pressing lines of unrooted bean seedlings into the wrong pots, propping himself up with one hand, pointing the blade of the trowel at her. What did they need cucumbers for? He'd never liked them. What did she want with marigolds? Useless things. Why had she planted only two varieties of tomato? Both got blight last year. How much had the pots cost? They could have made their own. Why bother with lettuce? Rabbit food. Sometimes if he had enough energy he'd broaden things out to include a critique of the raised beds. It drove Alison mad.

He was not an indoor man. He'd been working almost every day of his seventy-six years, and to him there was no value in a life without work. Not indoor work, but hard labour, physical graft, work which contained its own proof or contributed to the farm's own furthering. The sort of work where, at the end of the day, a material difference had been made: better fencing, fewer thistles. He acknowledged – reluctantly, almost furtively – his own diminishment, but how could someone retire from their own home?

It was no use at this stage in his life getting him to help with paperwork. That too was another of the tasks which had always been done by Alison, since Bert and computers disagreed. It was a traditional farming arrangement – Bert dealt with domestic issues, Alison with international ones, though even Alison's attempt to provide the public and diplomatic face of the farm faltered occasionally. After three days of waiting to speak to an actual human at the Rural Payments Agency about delays to the mid-tier Countryside Stewardship Scheme grant she had lost her temper and shouted something bad down the phone, a mistake which had earned her a frigid official silence and, two months later, a demand for partial repayment.

Either way it seemed that more time had to be spent in the

office than in the fields. In order to continue receiving the Basic Payment Scheme, Bert and Alison had either to prove they were still actively farming or hand the whole place over to David, who would in his turn have to provide similar proof. But David seemed destined for a life in Spain and Bert was too old. Which meant that it was Alison who became the farmer, and that she now assembled the feeders and mended the broken lambs. It was also she who ensured that no more than the maximum percentage permitted by regulations was rented out to others.

Bert felt the shift in responsibilities and, though he didn't speak of it, minded. On the one hand it was just a bit of bureaucratic finessing to keep the farm going. On the other, it was the difference between owning the farm, and not. Every time I saw him and asked him how he was doing, he'd say the same thing.

'Absolutely buggered. I been Ab-So-Lutely buggered.'

The weaker Bert got, the stronger his opinions. What he seemed most to resent was paying for work he had once been capable of doing himself. An electrician who turned up to solve a faulty connection was pursued from room to room by Bert complaining that there was nothing wrong with fifty-year-old wiring and that most things – brandy, fuses – improved with age. Two tree surgeons arrived to cut back the sycamore overstepping the lane and, though they cleaned every scrap of brash from the field, Bert stood below them and shouted over the whine of chainsaws that he found their prices a disgrace. The two men flicked down their ear defenders and carried on. It was Alison who was paying them.

'Cost me,' he said, glaring at the stump after they'd gone. 'Cost me a harm and a leg.'

Outside, Come Here had finally absconded to a better bitch and Bryn was getting old. He wasn't waiting at the door in the mornings any more and his daily surveys now had a scattered air, as if he'd just popped out for something but forgotten what it was. Bert and he would sit in the garden watching the sheep-dogs belonging to the young farmer who had taken the grazing – a temporary arrangement, according to Bert, just a couple of months. The new dogs were young and slippery, tucking themselves like hares into the long grass or rising from pools of shadow to ambush the running ewes. They were collies (one Welsh, one undecided) and still at an early stage in their professional development, keen to make a good impression, sticking their paws up for every job. When the new farmer paused to take a call on his mobile they'd sit watching his face like journalists after a story, and at the end of the day they'd all ride off down the lane, man and dogs in sunset harmony.

The tenant lived 20 miles away. He was a keen young farmer who had no land of his own but rented little blocks of land all over Wales. As the price of pasturage had risen, 'commuter farming' was becoming more common. Farmers had always patched fields together to make a complete holding, but over the past decade costs had reached the point where many had found it was only possible to run a successful stock farm by renting land a long way from home. Some people in the area were making round trips of almost 300 miles every day to get round their animals in different parts of the country.

Bert didn't talk much to him, or of him. Nor did he talk of the sheep any more. One by one all the foundations in his year began to crumble: lambing, shearing, weaning, tagging, the sales, the maintenance. What was left were the social points: Christmas, Easter, various birthdays, weddings, the summer barbecue up on the common. He talked more about humans, less about animals and often about machines: the old Volvo Estate he'd had for twenty-seven years, never a day out of sorts, 300,000 miles on the clock, sometimes passed its MOT, slight trouble with three of the doors, all of the windows and anything involving reverse but otherwise good as gold, nothing wrong with it that couldn't be sorted with a drop of oil or a lump hammer. When most of it had fallen off he drove what remained down to his old friend Morris in the garage. Morris stood in front of the bonnet. 'Putting it mildly, Bert,' he said, 'I never seen such a heap of shit in all my time.' Despite Bert's protestations the car was condemned as unfit for human transportation. The Howells got an Audi instead, which he hated.

With him, things only got worse. Because the lamb price had been low for a while a lot of farmers had been talking of planting apple trees – microbreweries, specialist cider. David had suggested putting a few saplings on the hill at the back of the house. It was stony in places, but there was good soil and it was south-facing.

'I said, "I never heard anything so stupid",' said Bert. '"What you going to do with seven trees? How are you going to get the apples from them? The bank's too steep." And he looked at me and he said, "Every idea I ever have, you tell me it's wrong. What am I supposed to do?"'

Bert was a canny man, honest enough to admit a wrong. He had shepherded the farm through nearly sixty years of hard weather, but he and his son could not get on. He was trying to treat David the way his father had treated him, though he understood that times had changed and David might have ways of doing things that were worth hearing.

'I won't stand for it,' he said, more and more often. 'I. Will. Not. Stand. For it.'

One of his kidneys had almost failed and the other one was struggling. A wrong thing had crept in and now the poison was seeping round his system. His circulation was slowing, dirtying with bad blood. He was supposed to have dialysis twice a week down at the county hospital but made it clear he didn't want to spend his time sat for hours in a wipe-clean recliner strapped to a machine directing his bodily functions. He understood absolutely the implications of that decision. If he was going to die, it was going to be at home. For the first time, there was slack skin round the muscles of his forearm.

'I feel so low,' he said, almost an aside, 'I could crawl under my own shoelaces.'

He looked rashy, wrong, all the contaminants unloosed. Whatever couldn't be expunged kept fouling his system, round and round, a dirty history. He couldn't pee, or he peed too much, or there was blood in it. His body was storing things it didn't need – given up on recycling, couldn't face the spring clean. It was beginning to tell him what the land already knew: he was no longer in charge. If he went outside now he could see the farm getting away from him. Scrap metal overflowed from the bins, feed boxes peeped from the brook, plastic sacks billowed in barbed wire. The gaps in the mortgage payments and magpies rattling from the telegraph poles were all shouting it loud and clear: other forces had taken over, stronger imperatives were now at work. The world was moving on.

7

Consumption

Out of town down a track to a half-timbered house standing gaunt in the winter landscape. An official-looking man muffled in a navy anorak and a branded wool hat is waiting with a clipboard in his hand. As we watch he goes round to the passenger seat of his car and checks his phone for the time.

'An auditor,' says Bill. His voice is low with unenthusiasm.

We pull up, get out, shake hands. The auditor is Reuben, a Spanish veterinarian from a company contracted to DEFRA whose job is to inspect other vets. He looks young and cold. As Bill opens the car boot he hovers just behind, peering over his shoulder at the contents of the plastic boxes while Bill extracts the necessary kit (blood tubes, syringes, callipers, paperwork, overtrousers, wellies) from the mobile dispensary within.

The kitchen door bangs. A man appears in well-used work clothes with a face underscored by time and humour. As he walks towards Bill, the two exchange a soundless glance through which course several decades of mutual understanding.

'Reuben,' Bill says, introducing Nigel. 'And Bella.'

While Bill scrubs down his boots and overtrousers we talk about the weather or the telly, something easy, something to keep everyone from dwelling on this particular procedural unease.

At present, any farmer with cattle must undergo testing for bovine tuberculosis (bTB). In low-risk eastern areas (Norfolk,

Lincolnshire, the Pennines) herds are tested less frequently, but in the high-risk areas they're tested at least once a year. The tests are done in two separate parts with a seventy-two-hour pause between the first and the second. At the end of the second day's testing the vet should be able to give the farmer the results and if the whole herd is declared clear then there should be no need for a retest. But if any of the cows fail or there are two consecutive 'inconclusive' results then those cows will be slaughtered, the whole herd will lose its TB-free status and no animals can be moved on or off the farm without a licence. This in turn has huge implications both for the herd's viability and for the future of the business. Any cattle from a TB-restricted farm, however healthy those individuals may be, immediately lose a sizeable chunk of their value. If the herd is considered very high-risk then there's the possibility that all the cattle may have to be killed.

Nigel has been clear for the last three years but this farm is surrounded by reactor herds. He has 220 beef cattle, almost all of which are Stabilisers – an American breed drawn from Simmental, Hereford, Gelbvieh and Red Angus stock. They're hardy and good-natured with broad expressive faces and rich brackenish colouring. Bill and Nigel shift an old oil barrel into position as a testing station and there's a bit of noise when we start moving the cattle around, but most go through the handling system without complaint.

For the first few minutes Reuben stands with his clipboard in front of him. Somehow the etiquette of all this seems awkward: the government auditor picking through a tick-list of items, the senior inspecting vet elaborately polite. As Nigel and the herdsman Ed herd the first group into the pen, Reuben huddles deeper into his scarf. Before he got this job, he said, watching Bill take out a box of latex gloves, he'd been doing abattoir testing, checking 400 cows a day – maybe a minute for each one and then a minute to look at each carcass. He hated it. Didn't like the people who worked at the abattoirs, didn't like the work. He didn't see himself lasting much longer at the TB work either. What he really wanted to do was go back to Spain and take up small-animal work again. What do you make of this? I asked. His shoulders lifted for a second and then hunched again. It's a job, he said. After fifteen minutes he left to go and inspect someone else.

For the rest of the first test day we stand there, corralling groups of animals into the race, pushing the headgate of the crush across as each cow goes through and noting down the relevant numbers. In between the numbers and the syringes, Bill and Nigel keep up a steady banter – children, news, local gossip. The two men have known each other for thirty-plus years, spend occasional Christmases together and are godparents to each other's children. The majority of that friendship is played out either on the farm or on the golf course. Both men are keen on sport and mercilessly competitive. In his youth Nigel had to make a choice between farming or playing football at county level, and Bill's idea of downtime is still an hour-long spin class after work, which means that much of their conversation revolves around insulting each other's golf scores.

Physically, they're entirely different. Bill is tall and clear, sparse as an old greyhound. He comes from a family of vets, grew up in Lanarkshire and remains a Calvinist in habit. Soft-spoken, intense, exhausted. In this area he is almost universally liked and respected for his commitment and professionalism. The staff at the practice are used to his insistence that late bloods must go to the lab that night rather than the following morning, that a herd's welfare must be fully checked at the same time as tests are done, that every possible piece of detection has been done to find the nature of a mystery equine stomach condition. So many clients ask for him that the staff have a code they add to the online diary – MBB: *Must Be Bill*. He survives on stress and high standards, is gentle and particular, won't say no to jobs, drives a car with the suspension of a wet mattress, is disastrous with technology and claims to be great at relaxing while admitting he only first became aware of holidays two years ago.

Nigel is also mid-fifties, but stockier, stubbed. A warm, expressive face scoured with lines across which moods flit like weather. He smiles easily, is furious easily, or troubled, or frustrated, or open, showing through an eyebrow or a line exactly where you stand. Soft as butter with his dogs and his daughters. At lunch he was thoughtful and open, though he is apparently famed for his temper. Back in the summer he had got so annoyed with a recalcitrant combine he'd challenged it to a fight. The combine won.

His relief at having Bill do the testing was evident. Nobody likes TB testing. It's repetitive, it's potentially risky, and even when a farm goes clear there's not much satisfaction in it. More experienced vets much prefer to be working on surgery or diagnostics, so from Bill's point of view this was as much a favour for an old friend as it was a day-and-a-half's concentrated work. And for all the comfort in familiarity and biscuits, the tension remained.

Nigel's farm stands in the middle of an epidemic. Tuberculosis has always existed, though it takes species-specific forms. In the UK it was for a long time seen as an affliction of the nineteenth century like typhoid or hysteria. In humans it became known as consumption for its habit of devouring from the inside, and it remains a steady killer in many countries, a disease associated with poverty and antibiotic resistance. But TB has never been exclusive to humans, and variants of the disease affect every species from elephants to goats. Confusingly, bovine TB can also be carried and spread by cats, deer, pigs, foxes and rodents, though not in general by horses or sheep. Because it took decades – centuries, in fact – to differentiate between the variant forms, transfer from cattle to humans did previously occur through contaminated cow's milk. Once the link was established the infection route was closed by pasteurisation or, in beef, through cooking. The only remaining source would be through the direct inhalation of bacteria from a sick animal.

Bovine TB is not as violently contagious as a disease like foot-and-mouth, but that means it glides from herd to herd slowly, quietly, down in the liminal spaces. And, unlike foot-and-mouth, you can't tell just by looking at a farm who's got it and who hasn't. This time the countryside isn't closed and there are no warning notices on gates. But since 2014 DEFRA has produced an interactive map of outbreaks showing both individual farm names and the overall number for the area. Though there has been statutory bTB testing on beef and dairy farms for thirty years or more the map still remains poxed with figures. To early December 2018 there were 2,404 restricted herds, a florid dotting broken mostly over the south and west. Nationwide bTB is probably holding steady, though within that there's huge local variation. At present the vast majority of outbreaks are in the South-west, the Midlands and Wales, partly because the arable flatlands of the east have fewer cattle herds and partly because the containment measures there have so far proved effective. Ireland managed to reduce its incidence of TB by a cull of all infected herds, and Scotland has kept its numbers down through a stringent testing regime. Even the DEFRA-funded TB Advisory Service concedes that current policy is 'holding TB at bay, not reducing … it'. In other words, this is not a disease under control. And, as one of their vets puts it, 'TB is political.'

The government would prefer us to think that it's being managed. Better still, they would like us not to think about it at all. Which, oddly enough, has been easy. It's the old magic trick: things vanish while you're looking somewhere else. If the wider public are aware of bovine TB they tend not to think of it in the context of cattle, but as something to do with badgers. Most of the sound and nearly all of the fury surrounding the disease has concentrated around the efficacy, or lack of it, of culling badgers, considered to be one of the main transmitters of the disease but also a UK protected species. No one's attention has been drawn to the numbers of cows – both healthy and diseased – which have been slaughtered because of bTB. Whatever your views on the badger cull, one of its consequences has been to elide the public gaze away from the other reality beneath.

And in truth, bTB has been bad for all species. In 2017 19,274 badgers were culled across the south-west counties of England. In the same year, over 43,000 cattle were classed as infected and slaughtered because of the disease. To date, 5.8 per cent of UK herds have either been under TB restrictions in the past or are currently under them – the highest incidence in Europe. Between 2008 and mid-2018, over a quarter of a million cattle from TB-restricted herds have been slaughtered. Some farmers, particularly those with pedigree cattle, keep closed herds, breeding only from their own stock and investing heavily in biosecurity measures. Even then, and despite doing everything they can to stay clean, they can find themselves infected when a fence breaks or a gate is left open or a deer wanders through. This is foot-and-mouth all over again, but pulled lengthwise through time.

And for every misfortune, there is an opportunity. Some areas are now so prone to the disease that a few people have started 'farming TB'. In other words, they have been restricted for so long they can neither get clear nor get out, so they have adapted their farming techniques around the restrictions and become Approved Finishing Units, buying only from restricted herds. Even farms which do continue under bTB restrictions can claim compensation for any slaughtered cattle. Which, though lower than the market price, is not insignificant – in early 2019 the pay-out for a single year-old beef bull was nearly £4,000, and a two-year-old dairy cow on her first lactation £1,555.

There might be a few opportunists who have managed to turn TB to their own benefit, but generally no one wins. Not the badgers (there is the official cull, and then there is the not-even-slightly-official alternative), not the taxpayer (who in 2017 paid nearly £100 million in tests and compensation), not the farmers (whose job is to rear healthy animals). And most of all, not the cattle.

All farmers, whether of stock or crops, have to brace against the random unkindnesses of disease and bad weather. But this, for many, is the end. Many farmers find the stress and grief of TB too much, the judgement that never relents, the threat of reinfection the final straw. One by one individual farmers are taking this as a cue to get out of the market altogether. In 1974, there were 15.4 million cattle in this country. Since then there have been three major disease outbreaks (BSE, foot-and-mouth and bTB) as well as several minor ones. The national herd now stands at around 10 million – a fall of over a third in four decades. It is perhaps an interesting irony that it may not be pressure from campaigners or a decline in the market which leads to a reduction in the consumption of beef, but the sheer sadness of a half-secret disease. They don't call it a TB breakdown for nothing.

Down a scabby lane and through a gate with one hinge to a yard scattered with buildings. There's a yellow forklift running across the yard, piles of cable wormed round the fences and a trim of baggy black baler plastic billowing round the edges of the sheds. This place looks more like an industrial estate than a farm, though appearances are designed to be deceiving – it's one of the richest farms in Pembrokeshire.

It's run by Clive Grinnell, his daughter Kayleigh and his nephew Taylor. Clive appears first, an easy, quiet figure in his mid-seventies wearing an old Claas overall and a worn brown muffler. As the large-animal vet Dan Sowerby works through his car-boot preparations, Clive explains that until recently this place was a dairy farm. For thirty-nine years he milked cows twice a day, a requirement as fixed as the rise of the tides. The only times he ever left the farm were to go to the local livestock market, and when that moved, he didn't really leave the farm at all. Like many from that generation he lived according to the principle that some things in life (death, milking) were not optional.

But then two things happened. First, the price of milk settled a long way south of the cost of production. And secondly, in 2015, both their beef and dairy herds went down with TB.

This time, the work was done in a big strawed-down shed with a small tin milking hut in the centre. One side of the space was partitioned off with gates and arranged to ensure the cattle came down the side into the race and from there out to the other end. Because of the farm's past, many of the cattle have been bred from dairy stock which, though used to being handled, can sometimes be trickier than their beef counterparts. These seem to come from every breed known – Limousin, Charolais, Simmental, Hereford, Red Poll, Holstein-Friesian, Angus, Shorthorn, Jersey – anything, everything, all at once; 1,000-kilo dirty-curled bulls next to wide-eared newborns in impeccable russet. They are as various in colour as they are in expression and temperament: patched or belted, mottled or long-haired, horned or polled. One cow's old body sags off her like dustsheets over furniture, while beside her a beefier teen stands rounded as a hill. A fox-red heifer waits half-outlined in light as weak winter sun shines through the hairs on her back while bullocks stare at us through albino-blonde eyelashes or shift knobby-kneed from foot to foot.

Kayleigh waits silently at the back urging the grouped cattle into the race while Dan positions himself by the head of the crush. Taylor is talking, his hand on the lever. Despite the reassuring bulk of the milking hut behind us the mood is uneven. It's clear that the animals do not feel safe and that they feel no safety from the humans around them. This particular farm has been under a TB restriction continuously for the past two years, which means all the cattle have to be tested on a constant sixty-day rotation. Which means in turn that all the Grinnells' cattle except the youngest calves know only too well what a TB test entails.

On the neck of each cow Dan clips two square patches, one above the other. Pinching the skin in each patch, he measures the thickness with callipers, calls out the cow's tag number and then two figures indicating the skin thickness, then injects the upper one with avian TB virus and the lower with bovine TB. Once I'd made a note of the figures Clive would open the gate so the cow could join its companions.

All of which sounds like a nice straightforward procedure. But in practice, cows are cows and people are people and however expert the vet, the crush gates would jam or the last cow wouldn't go into the pen or someone's phone rang. The Grinnells' animals do not arrive in orderly lines but in bundles, rearing and pouncing, shaking their heads. Some stand quietly, pinned between a jolting calf and the heifer wrestling in front, while others come hurtling out of the crush, hot-eyed, kicking like springs. A couple of heifers have jagged gashes from ripped ear tags while others just stand there, head down, trying to work out the meaning of us. Some – knowing that they might be injected near the throat – lower themselves to their knees as they enter and dip their heads like devotees in prayer. Some of the smaller ones try to reverse back up the race or nod vigorously, picking their moment just as Dan reaches to pinch the skin. One – a patient old milker – has a wall eye, others have sores or traces of blood on their necks. Cows twitch their heads away, trapping Dan's hand between the bars or the handle of the crush flicked upwards, almost smacking him in the face. Groups of tested animals stand around the circular hay feeder, occasionally touching noses.

Taylor meanwhile has other things in mind. He leans against the hut and raises his voice. Car drivers, for a start. Rude, they were. Stupid. Didn't understand tractors, didn't know the first thing about farming, always trying to overtake. Suicidal, most of them. Dangerous to other road users. And the worst? Rudest of all? Old women. Old women in Micras. Can't drive. Can't even see, most of them. So low down they could barely reach the steering wheel. And middle-aged ones. Women late to pick up their kids from school, beeping at him, shouting as they overtook, driving these great SUVs with two foot of ego on each side. In the past he might have pulled in to let them pass but, not going to lie, he'd given up bothering. Sick of never being thanked, no respect.

'They should be rounded up and shot, I reckon.'

Who?

'All of them. Women. I'n't none of them can drive.'

He glanced up. 'Present company. But what most of them shouldn't be on the roads.'

Finding a lack of comeback on this point, he moved on. To better emphasise his points, he had appropriated Dan's crook and was now poking it through the bars of the race, trying to push a couple of the cows backwards. The cows, having nowhere to go, looked confused.

For a start, there was the pathetic compensation levels offered to TB-restricted farmers ('… Don't even … Barely worth claiming. Not even half the price I paid most of the time. They're trying to cheat us what we should get by pushing it right down') to vets ('… Do you honestly think these people want to get rid of TB and be out of a job?') to vegans ('tree-huggers') and DEFRA ('… Trouble is, most of 'em never been outside London. All they know what to do is sit in an office making regulations. No understanding of the real world, none at all. I'n't what one of them would last ten minutes on a real farm'), via (for my benefit) a run-down of cattle breeds ('Simmentals, they're nasty' – pointing at a bullock who has been staring fixedly at us for the last ten minutes – 'Proper vicious streak. Plenty of farmers killed by Sims.' The bullock lowers his head. 'Lims, they're not much better. Worst' – poking at a cow the size of a Portakabin – 'is Charolais. Look at 'im. Mean') and thence to one of his tenants ('… Never did a stroke of work, laziest man I ever saw, and I'm a Christian').

As Taylor talked, Kayleigh and Clive carried on herding the animals through the race, silent and unprovoked. Occasionally, changing one pen of animals for another, they would call an instruction or whistle a command, but otherwise they gave no sign either of registering that Taylor was talking or that he was in any way connected to them. Even so, Taylor's commitment to making up for any perceived conversational shortfall meant that he was often slow to bang the gate shut at the back, meaning that one cow would turn and Dan would have to test the cow behind first.

In fact, so determined was Taylor's flow of opinions I started wondering if perhaps this wasn't a way of getting the farm TB-free. If, through the strategic overuse of his views,

Taylor could only distract Dan for long enough, then either Dan might overlook a couple of cows that needed testing, or I might muddle up the numbers on the tag sheet, substituting a clean animal for a reactor, or the animals themselves would get so upset that they charged us, thus transforming this scene into a very different sort of statistic.

From a farmer's point of view the impulse to finesse the tests must sometimes be difficult to resist. It isn't just that the financial consequences of going down with bTB are so great, it's the less obvious things – the taint of contamination, the loom of the sixty-day deadlines, the smack of official disapproval. The judgement of their neighbours, unexpressed but omnipresent. Trying to find space to keep reactors separated from healthy cattle, trying to find enough money to keep cattle which would normally have been sold. The inconvenience of two days out of the schedule every time. Condemning cattle which appear healthy, or which are in calf. Vets, officials, inspectors on the farm. Testing, testing. The majority just get on with it – have the tests, receive the results, deal with the consequences. A very small number do their best to game the system.

At the other farm the previous day the lists had tallied almost exactly. Here, they seem to bear only a mild acquaintance to the cows passing before us. There are newborn calves who do have numbers and mid-size teens who don't, cows whose tags on one ear do not answer to the tags on the other, cows with unlisted numbers and listed numbers with no apparent cows. Despite Dan's best efforts to keep the testing on track, the going is slow. Some animals have to be hunted down or separated out into smaller groups. The bull – coronet of kiss-curls, surly punkish glare – has a pen of his own and an uncooperative set to his ears. Even once bribed with a bucket of pellets and pinned in a metal headlock, he pulls and twitches. Dan can't find an easy position. The syringe arcs and vanishes.

This, says Dan – large-animal vet practice – is one of the most dangerous professions in the UK after farming itself. There is a weary note in his voice. Animals don't – can't – understand that the ominous needle/drench/pill/knife/syringe is intended to make them better. Horses kick or rear or buck, cows defend their calves, bulls charge. In some quarters a certain machismo still attaches to the profession. Farmers sometimes find it entertaining to test a rookie vet by sending them into a pen with an animal they know to be dangerous. And vets still say yes to jobs they suspect will be risky, partly because if they don't do it someone else will, partly because it's not the animal's fault, and partly because they also succumb to that same phlegmatic it-happens bravado. The risk of being struck or bitten by a horse is high, and Dan himself was double-barrelled (both hooves) by a cow not long ago – 'I'm a big man, but it pinged me across the shed like a pea from a shooter. If I'd put my head down a second before, it would have snapped my neck.'

And things are not getting any easier. For every refinement in safety (better handling systems, improvements to machinery and to medicine itself) there is a corresponding increase in risk. The recent trend for double-muscling – cattle bred with twice the amount of lean muscle – meant that the size of calves increased accordingly, which in turn meant that some breeds became almost unable to give birth naturally. Once a red-letter rarity, Caesareans became a norm. A fully qualified large-animal vet will sometimes be expected to perform surgery or a post-mortem wherever that animal has taken itself. All the older practice vets talk of doing five, ten, fifteen Caesareans in the space of a few days – ten operations performed while tucked into a hard corner with a panicky cow. They are also expected to be on call for emergencies at least one night a week, and depending on the size of the practice one or two weekends a month. And this is not the old James Herriot story of single animals on small farms. What vets are treating now is the herd itself: bulk-testing procedures like bTB or generalised checks for Johne's disease. They're thinking not just of the health of an individual animal, but how that impacts on the strength of the collective.

All the senior vets at this rural practice are as much absorbed in directing the future form of the flocks or herds under their supervision as in treating laminitis or rasping teeth. It's increasingly specialised. Some just do equine, some just do bTB, very few still do full general practice. It's cold or it's rainy. It's boring, badly lit, risky, rewarding, fiddly, disheartening, joyful, filthy. To stick at it you need bravado and stoicism, a real commitment to animal health, a knack for human psychology. You get to know many of your clients very well – perhaps too well, sometimes. You know them when they're stressed, or stressed but trying not to show it, or so stressed they lash out, sometimes at you. You know them when it all goes wrong or once comes right. You become the bearer of bad news or good, unravelling long-made plans, confirming suspicions, condemning, reprieving. You know how farmers react when there's been a death in the family. You spend a lot of time in a car. Which is why many new vets now qualify for large-animal practice, have a look round and decide that maybe they prefer clipping cats' claws after all.

While Taylor moved from the cost of branded biscuits to the price utility companies charged for rerouting cables ('I laughed. I'm not going to lie, I laughed. It's like they think we're stupid'), Dan moved through the whole herd, chasing up anomalies, querying discrepancies. He noted any cows with missing tags, treated those with torn ears and made sure that the list and the reality tallied. The cattle stayed restive but subdued, huddled together as they came out of the crush.

This particular large-animal practice now does 150,000 bTB tests a year – half the work in South Wales – with an additional six vets who do nothing but test full-time. This isn't just a temporary response to a temporary issue: this is a complete micro-economy, a growth industry with its own replicating cell structure. DEFRA pays the basic price of testing, but most of the additional costs have to be met by the farmers, which means that TB has become a source of income for the practice. That in turn breeds its own ambivalence: the advantage of a constant, constantly increasing stream of chargeable time associated with TB versus the grim banality of the work itself.

All of this – this accretion of time and labour and paperwork and tests and crushes, the phials and procedures and inspections and ordinary human misery, the drag on farmers and farming, the unspoken emotional attrition – this is the silt of many years' experience. It has taken years for cattle in this part of the world to learn that people just want to stick needles in them, years for the infrastructure of finishing units and red markets to build up, years for the cows and the farmers to take the punches and take the punches and then fall down. BTB has been running for more than three decades, and in the high-risk areas it has kept livestock farming in a state of lockdown, suffocating hope or progress.

But it was another disease, a sharper, more acute viral infection, which has come to define much of farming today.

The first intimation came on 19 February 2001. By the time evidence of foot-and-mouth had been verified in twenty-seven pigs at an Essex abattoir, the disease had already been transported round a further fifty-seven farms, scattering infection from Galloway to Devon. It took a further four days before the circulation of animals around the UK was halted. On 16 March, Nick Brown – then Labour Secretary of State for the Ministry of Agriculture, Fisheries and Food (MAFF) – initially announced the slaughter of all animals (not just cloven-hooved ones) within a three-mile exclusion zone, and then 'clarified' that to include only sheep and pigs, not cattle. A week later the contiguous cull policy was introduced, meaning that all stock on any clean farms adjoining outbreak areas had to be slaughtered within forty-eight hours. But this was spring, which meant that on many farms lambs or calves were killed within minutes of birth. Ministry officials arrived on many farms in biohazard suits and shot everything on four legs. In many cases, the corpses – and their unborn or newborn calves or lambs – were left for up to a week before collection. Though protocols from previous outbreaks insisted on a total ban on movement and a cull of all infected animals within twenty-four hours of confirmation, at the time no minister referred to the earlier inquiries' recommendations.

Foot-and-mouth is itself a debateable disease. It's a virus with the capacity to affect all cloven-hooved animals, starting with a fever and becoming most noticeable in the blisters which form and burst in the mouth and on the feet of the animal. It is not transmissible to humans, but is highly infectious between species (cow to ewe, pig to calf), and between animals of the same species. The only aspect of foot-and-mouth over which there is no dispute is its speed of contagion. Nor is it a new thing – between 1929 and 1953 there wasn't a single year when the UK was completely free of foot-and-mouth disease. Some point out that its effects can be mild, that animals can and do recover from it, and that other countries regard foot-and-mouth in the same way we think of chickenpox in children. Many regard it as an economic disease, a killer of livelihoods degrading a beast's physical value but requiring no need either for vaccination or for culling. Others see it as a cross between leprosy and the plague – animals with tongues and teats so blistered they can't eat, drink or suckle their young. Farmers reported cows rotting from the inside, reeking and agonised, for whom the slaughterman's gun became a too-late release. In its full-blown form foot-and-mouth is acutely, visibly painful. None of those who dealt with infected animals during the 2001 outbreak was in any doubt that they were suffering.

At a time of year when many farmers should be at their busiest, there was nothing to do. Because of the movement restrictions, those farms which hadn't yet been culled were unable to move their stock from field to field, meaning the animals lost condition and started to starve. A further 'welfare cull' was introduced to take out animals not fat enough for the butcher. The grass sallowed from overgrazing. The common land grew bracken and the lambing sheds stayed empty. On many culled farms MAFF imposed a ban on cleaning while Whitehall squabbled itself into a frenzy over costs. In parts of Cumbria, craft shop owners reported that a few farmers were appearing at the till with china figurines of ewes. Nobody left the farm and nobody arrived except people carrying guns or bad news.

In the big field on Rise Farm there's an old ash tree at the top of an outcrop which has stood through more than a century of westerlies. The field is steep at its lower end, bordered by a hedgling of elder and hawthorn. At the higher end the lane runs through the farmyard and round towards the common land. The ash tree is where they burned the animals.

This farm didn't have foot-and-mouth, but one of the neighbouring farmers had sheep on a field near a confirmed outbreak, which meant that Rise, along with all the other farms on the hill, was put down as a 'dangerous contact'. On Easter Monday 2001, 23 Hereford Friesian suckler cows, their calves, 60 fattening cattle, one Charolais bull, 450 Suffolk cross ewes and their lambs, 50 ewe lambs and 10 Suffolk tups were slaughtered.

Bert was given notice on Good Friday. Two days later a line of bio-suited slaughtermen stood at the top of the lane. In the shed he and Alison were pulling new lambs out of ewes even as the Ministry insisted they round up what they had and had it shot at close quarters. Birth to death in a blink of light. Having done what was demanded, Bert finally lost it, got one of the MAFF liaison officers up against a wall and told him that if he didn't have the whole lot shot and off the farm by 1 p.m., he'd no longer be held responsible for his own actions. Then he went into the farmhouse, closed the curtains and cried like a child. Within forty-eight hours, half the stock was burned in the field beneath the ash while the other half was loaded into tipper trucks and taken to landfill. All the animals had been healthy.

MAFF field officers felt themselves as the enemy. Perhaps not blamed, but hated all the same. The veteran journalist Jon Snow compiled a special report for Channel 4 on the crisis and later wrote of that time: 'Air crashes, road accidents, riots, the odd murder, nothing in twenty-five years of reporting domestic news had ever prepared me for the scale of human trauma I experienced that mad March weekend last year. It was unutterably brutal.'

Anyone who lived or worked near one of the affected areas will remember the placid spring horizons spiked with upraised legs, or the ghastly, delicious drift of smoky bacon threading between the woods. By mid-April, 10,000 vets were involved in fighting the outbreak as well as an unknown number of extra slaughtermen. In the worst-affected areas, 100,000 animals a day were being culled. Sites for the incineration of the resulting animal carcasses were overwhelmed. In many areas pyres were built and fuelled with a form of coal which only smouldered slowly. One farmer said that after two months of 'incineration', it was still possible to read the ear tags on his cattle. It was a hallucinatory, sleep-deprived time, the countryside quarantined, farms barricaded. The things which once seemed so innocent – land, animals, nature – were now contaminated. If cities had always represented resistance and dirt, then the places beyond meant cleanliness. The countryside was still supposed to be the refuge of truth but now nature too had fallen, and if nature fell then there could no longer be nothing good in the world. Several farmers noted that as they shot the animals, the birds fell silent.

By the time the army first arrived in Cumbria at the end of March there was a backlog of 70,000 sheep to be burned. Two weeks later a single site – Great Orton in Cumbria – was dealing with the daily slaughter of 18,000 animals. The army's involvement marked the turning point. Under Brigadier Alexander Birtwistle, slaughtered animals were moved off farms within twenty-four hours. Recognising that political dithering was only adding to the trauma, he came up with a clear strategy and executed it to the letter. In the end the epidemic lasted for thirty-two weeks and led to the deaths of around 10 million animals. North Cumbria alone lost 70 per cent of its animals. The economic loss to the country was calculated to be somewhere in the region of £9 billion; the psychological loss remains incalculable.

Inevitably there is still disagreement about what could have been done differently: a lack of discretion in applying a policy which kept changing, errors and defensiveness, poor communication: all the usual charges. Those four petrified days in February between identification and lockdown were later thought to be one of the deciding factors. And however apparently logical the contiguous cull, it was one thing for farmers to watch animals who were plainly diseased being shot, but absolutely another to accept the killing of hundreds of healthy newborns just because they were within three miles of a suspected case.

The governmental reflex was to retreat behind a fortifying wall of paper – three reports this time, adding to the pile from previous episodes. The details had changed (in the time since the 1967 outbreak, the country had lost a third of its farms and half of its auction markets) but the essentials had not.

'We seem destined to repeat the mistakes of history,' wrote Dr Iain Anderson, chair of the 2002 government inquiry, in the introduction to his report. While noting that Whitehall officials had done their best, 'One finding of this Inquiry has been the extent of the breakdown of trust between many of those affected directly or indirectly, and their Government.' After sweeping unchecked over the headlines for months, news of the outbreak was finally displaced by 9/11 and, for the non-farming community at least, vanished into the list of Grim Things About 2001. By the following spring shops and B&Bs in the affected areas had reopened, footpaths no longer carried Keep Out signs and tourists meandered back, at first tentatively and then in ordinary hordes. For those on a family holiday, there was nothing amiss. The grass still grew and there were still sheep in the fields. It still rained.

But for those who lived there it was a different matter. Even at the time it was clear that one of the consequences of the outbreak had been to lengthen the distance between town and country. It wasn't just a matter of the physical barriers (the Keep Out signs, the movement ban), but the psychological ones as well. A black market in rumours sprang up. Who, and how many, had contaminated their own stock? Who had brought the disease in the first place, and who infected their neighbours? Whose tup had been seen through the back window of a family caravan taking a covert jaunt cross-country, and who had burned their animals with battery acid to make them look diseased? Friendly vets had sometimes given farms with borderline results a choice: declare it as an outbreak and take the compensation, or keep stock which would eventually go to market anyway. Some farmers stayed viable and some took the loss. Many grew more mistrustful of a Ministry they'd never liked anyway. Guilt, or a pending election, or a desire just to be shot of the problem, enforced a savage official generosity. Stories still abound of compensation at double or treble the market rate, pay-outs for beasts which had never actually existed, payments for pedigrees which were in fact mules, new cars, tractors, garages.

The distance between farmers and government reached unreachable, an impacted carapace of contempt and anger (stories still linger of the MAFF official who asked a farmer what sex his bull was). As for those who lived in cities, they hated the sight of the pyres but didn't really get it. Why were farmers so upset about their animals dying? They were going to kill them anyway. Why were they crying over a heap of dead lambs? Everyone knew farmers only loved money. Why were they so angry? Farmers were always angry.

Time passed. The country moved on and paid the bill. People began worrying about other things – Iraq, Soham. The seasons turned. Perhaps some might notice that the cows returning to the fields were now a different breed, or that farm-gate conversations always seemed to lurch every time a tipper went past. Previously mixed farms now grew only sheep or weeds, while others planted crops of caravans. Village high streets semaphored For Sale signs. Some people took the disease as a cue to get out of farming altogether, some to carry on as before and some as an opportunity. A few took the money, bought themselves a house in the village and retired, giving a handful of tenants a chance to get started or to upgrade. But for all the heartache, the majority of farmers kept farming – either because they were too old to retrain, or because the land had long ago hooked them in and would never let go.

Up at Rise Farm, Bert and Alison gave up cattle and pigs. Bert loved the cows, but had found it impossible to keep on. Banned because of movement restrictions from bringing his part-share bull back onto the farm for the cows, Bert had rung the Ministry. They said there were no concessions possible: if he wanted pregnant cows, then their recommendation was that he hire a clean bull and kill it after.

'I said, "I'm not getting a disposable bull." You'd never think an educated chap would come out with something like that.'

Most farmers restocked, burying hope under busyness. Just once in a while, the effects might poke out from underneath: two or three suicides close to the cull's anniversary, a few farmers showing symptoms similar to PTSD, a shooting ten years after the event.

To the rest of the country foot-and-mouth is, at most, a very distant memory. To many farmers it's both the end, and a beginning. Though the Covid-19 outbreak of 2020 produced its own echo (the paranoia, the lockdown, the endless washing, the anonymised figures in biohazard visors, the governmental instructions, the race for compensation), there's a difference. For Britain's urban population Covid came out of the sky, a once-in-a-century event, random as a meteorite. For its rural population, Covid looked more like a continuum, a thing to add to the land's long list of adaptations. During the nineteenth century the UK dealt with regular outbreaks of cholera, typhoid, diphtheria and TB. The west of Ireland is still crossed by the roads to nowhere built by the starving in exchange for food, and during the twentieth century Britain dealt with outbreaks of smallpox and polio as well as the Spanish flu epidemic of 1918. Trees, meanwhile, have been hit by everything from Dutch elm disease to *phytophthora ramorum*, and foot-and-mouth was only the worst of an almost routine set of livestock disorders: swine fever, brucellosis, scrapie, BVD (Bovine Viral Diarrhoea), Schmallenberg, orf, BSE …

But there was something about the 2001 foot-and-mouth outbreak which seemed uniquely destructive. In many areas everyone still refers back: that was the time that so-and-so died, or the tenancy changed, or they sold the last of the horses. 2001 produced more than one Ground Zero.

All of which provides both the context and the contrast to bovine TB. There have always been epidemics. Some, like foot-and-mouth, are sudden, and others, like TB, slip like contagion slow under the grass.

Two days later Bill went back to do the second part of the TB test at Nigel's farm. Reuben the auditor was there waiting by his car again. This time Nigel was more taciturn, shoving a couple of the cows into the pen, slamming the gates home, and though he was doing his absolute best not to swear within my earshot the effort was almost turning him blue.

The cows too seemed more snappish. Once out, a couple of the more opinionated heifers stood in the yard mooing back at the rest of the herd, urgent, peremptory calls, a kind of command. As they moved through the race, Bill ran his fingers over the little shaven patches on their necks. If he felt a lump or any thickening in the skin, he measured it and noted the change. A reactor would show a larger increase in the measurement around the bovine TB injection than it would around the avian one.

'Do you ever feel the temptation …?' I asked Bill during a pause.

'... Yes,' he said, picking up the line of thought. 'You do sometimes feel like squeezing a bit harder on the callipers. But if it's over, it's over – you can't deny the results. However much you'd sometimes like to.'

The second part of the test usually goes more quickly, but the day was freezing – frost on the northern edges of the shed, ice on the feed bin – and Bill began to lose feeling in his gloved hands. As he fielded calls outside, Nigel and Ed sat in the kitchen, raiding the biscuit tin. Ed sat at the breakfast bar, head bent over his phone, a big lad with a canny trick of vanishing in plain sight.

We pull on boots again and return to the yard for the final few animals. The tension remains, rising.

Under the shaven patches, a couple of the cows have visible lumps, while on others the skin has thickened invisibly. Bill goes along the line feeling each animal's neck, up and down between the cows and the calves.

In the end, though several of Nigel's animals were either very close to the line or on it, none of them was over. The herd was clear, as was the depth and strength of Nigel's relief. In a high-risk area surrounded by positive farms, a negative result said something for Nigel's stockmanship.

At the farm in Pembrokeshire, Dan was back to do the second part of the test. As expected, there were reactors within the herd, and it did not lose its restricted status.

8

Remote Control

Bert died.

A few days later the village assembled.

As a queue of cars made its way slowly down the hill, men wedged into unfamiliar suits stood smiling solemnly while women tiptoed across the grass, pulling down skirt hems and brushing the dust from their husbands' collars. It was September but warm, and the grass was dry and there were birds in the trees. The church was full to overspilling, but someone had rigged up a PA system and the latecomers stood with their hands clasped, listening to the service from outside. A slight breeze came and went, blowing across the speakers. Those inside could hear the singing from the churchyard, a live echo which in the half-beat delay seemed somehow very old, a call and response sounding from the walls themselves.

On a wobbly projector, the family showed a timeline of Bert's life. There was the old thresher, a shed-sized lump of unintelligible wood into which the corn and – later – the part-time jobs of six men were fed. There was Bert on horseback and Bert with one of the tups. There was Bert with Ron, Bert with pigs, Alison and Bert on their wedding day. Horses and carts. Several dogs. Bert on the tractor helping to dig the electricity company's vans out of a snowdrift. A rare, startling image of

Bert on a beach, face and arms tanned brown, legs as pale as the moon. Bert giving the speech at his daughter's wedding, the cows, Bert on a market day, a barbecue, Christmas dinners with a home-grown turkey. Alison told his life slowly and with humour. The last picture was him sat on the quad bike with his eighteen-month-old granddaughter perched on his lap, both of them grinning like they really really meant it.

There, between the lines of this one man, was the whole history of twentieth-century British farming, from the all-out ploughing of the Second World War to the Millennium bonfires. Bert was born in 1937, and there were old family photos of him, his sisters and an evacuee called Sheila who went native and stayed for six years. Rise during the war, the fields turned over to sugar beet but the top of the hill left bare. Unfamiliar horses collared for ploughing. Bert clutching a scythe the same height as himself. Harvest suppers and shearing competitions, pictures of revolutionising new machinery and, within the span of a few photographs, the slide of that same machinery down to the status of antiques. The turning of the years was marked not so much by the seasons as by the photographic technology (black and white, colour, digital) and the farming practices (hand-stooked corn to rectangular bales, rectangular bales to round ones). Cider-making from the farm orchard, men with lurchers or ferrets arriving to kill rabbits in the days before myxomatosis. Sheep dipping, baling the bracken for bedding, eggs for sale. Most of it was monotonous physical work and – since Bert's father was a great believer in child labour – almost all unpaid. A few of the post-war pictures showed the full-fat farm working with a line of people all fed from the land. Milk came from the Jersey cows, heat from the woods, water from the spring and money from the government.

Sometimes the photographs were there to mark a significant moment (levelling the ground for the big shed), but mostly the things in the foreground were people and animals. And behind them was the land. The drop down into the valley or some familiar corner – the pond, the shed, the garden, the side of the farmhouse, the wonky gable end, Bert standing by a newly pointed wall. Beyond that, sometimes visible only as an arrangement of greys, was the wider view, the line of Wales, the hill, the flat geometry of the conifer plantation. Reversing back through the 1970s the old ash still had its central limb and the broken-down bit in the wall had repaired itself. The road sprung new tarmac, then potholes, then potholes in different places. The cottage acquired serrated rows of fruit and veg, or an extra lean-to. There were newly planted plum trees in the orchard and a workshop facing east. Behind them the old buildings sulked in the mud. The farm expanded, stretching out along the side of the hill. Pylons marched up the far horizon. And always there was the hills and the grass and the river, and they hadn't changed at all.

And somehow it seemed as if the pictures had spun back even further, reeling out of photography and back to the nineteenth century – etchings, drawings, oak-gall ink – it wouldn't have been much to see Bert there, still crouched in the farrowing pen. The removal of that badgerish presence buttressing the farm against change seemed bewildering. He *was* the farm. He was its leader and its head of state. He had spent forty years at the head of his own principality, patrolling the borders, repelling invaders, consolidating the economy. His foreign policy might have been conservative (voted UKIP, hated ramblers), and his views on social issues were frankly terrifying (keen on the reintroduction of corporal punishment and the re-criminalisation of homosexuality), but if he couldn't always guarantee anything like democracy among his subjects, then he had at least tried to offer a reliable kind of dictatorship. If the doctors had opened him up, Bert's blood would have flowed the same ferrous red as the earth beneath, and the same fine flow of pollen, lanolin and muck would have aerated both his first breath and his last.

Even so, and despite what the photographs said, it had been Alison running things for a while. Since he'd been ill she, David or a rotating crew of extras, handymen and neighbours had been doing the morning rounds. She was the one who haggled with several mutually uncommunicative sets of doctors over Bert's care. In addition to making sure that food arrived on the table she completed the forms, picked up the prescriptions, made the appointments and kept the diary, the farm's most sacred text. The diary was there so everyone knew what they were doing and when, and had thus always been the source of frequent internecine skirmishes. In the months before Bert died, the appointments it contained had moved from mostly practical to partly medical. For a long while he had been there but not there, visible mostly as an absence – the dent in the sofa, the upended copy of the *Daily Mail*, the TV remote control. Most evenings he was the empty place at the head of the table, asleep by 9 p.m. before rising punctually at 3 a.m. From his daughter's point of view the bonus to this schedule was that he was an excellent childminder, waking at roughly the same times as a toddler and – from a lifetime of lambing – expert with a bottle feed. The downside was that his temper hadn't improved.

Bert was gone, but the land continued. The whole point of a stock farm was that it had many lives, and – give or take one less or one more – they carried on. There were animals who weren't putting on weight, and someone wanted to cut the third crop of hay for the anaerobic digester. The Ministry required its weekly feed of forms and the SFP was coming up for renewal. The Land Rover needed a new gearbox and it was time to get the hedges cut again. Bert had defined Rise's direction for forty years or more, and now it was up to the next generation to make a future from it. But what *was* the future for farms like these?

Agriculture, they say, is the sector most profoundly affected by Europe, and thus the sector most marked by Brexit. Eighty per cent of it is governed or regulated by legislation from the EU. For almost a half century British farming has been paying with European money, selling along European lines and – to its apparent disgust – playing by European rules. It might occasionally have been an unhealthy relationship, but even before joining the Community in 1973 and the 1975 referendum to remain within it, it was always a close one. Even so, during the long run-up to the 2016 referendum, the farming vote swung from Remain to Leave – a shift which seemed bewildering for a sector so apparently reliant on Brussels.

Or that's the view at first glance. But to read that vote as a betrayal of global economic reality is to miss the history in this, only some of which has anything to do with Europe. As much as anything, it was a rejection of an agricultural policy so necrotic as to be past saving.

Richard Whyte is a former ministerial speechwriter, led three major reviews for the Treasury and the Department of Transport and at various times has held positions at both the Foreign and Cabinet Offices. At DEFRA he worked under five ministers for seven years, and at the Department of Justice is now in charge of a wide-ranging review of the criminal justice system. In other words, he is a civil servant of sufficient talent, experience and seniority to be permitted once in a while to speak the truth.

I arranged to meet him at his office in Lionheart House, an anonymous building hidden beneath scaffolding near

Millbank. He's tall, cheerful and looks, if not exactly agricultural, then not totally urban either. He must be in his
mid-fifties, has sandy hair arranged in a sort of flat white Afro
– flat because he keeps lacing his hands together and squish-
ing the top of his head while he's thinking – and an easy, open
manner. The only thing about him which is not at all rural
are his hands, as tapering and elegant as the hands of Aubrey
Beardsley. It was a useful meeting from which I gleaned three
key points: that whatever farmers think of government, the
reality is worse, that no one at DEFRA has ever actually been to
the country, and that attitudes to it are split along party lines:
Tories want to shoot the wildlife while Labour would rather
shoot the inhabitants.

In some form or another there has been a government
department responsible for agriculture since 1889. Before that
there was no need. Only landowners could become MPs so
therefore the interests of MPs and landowners were one and
the same. The millions of smallholders, tenants and crofters
who did the actual physical work on the land had no vote and
thus no power. Agricultural improvement societies – also led by
landowners – were also responsible for bringing in new tech-
nologies or changing the way land was arranged, which meant
it wasn't until well after the large-scale movement towards the
cities during the Industrial Revolution that there was any real
split between the interests of farmers (rural) and those of the
governing classes (urban).

By the turn of the twentieth century government dealt with
farmers through policy and farmers dealt with government
through the newly formed National Farmers' Union (NFU).
In fact, the department responsible for agriculture has gone
through several different namings, the sum of which provides
a handy thumbnail guide to its past. First it was the Board of
Agriculture, then it was the Board of Agriculture and Fisheries,

then it became the Ministry of Agriculture and Fisheries which during both wars was subdivided into local War Agricultural Executive Committees (War Ags) plus a separate Ministry of Food. Following the end of war it turned into the Ministry of Agriculture, Fisheries and Food (MAFF) before being rebranded following the ignominy of the 2001 foot-and-mouth outbreak as the Department for Environment, Food and Rural Affairs (DEFRA). The Secretary of State responsible for farming was once the Agriculture Minister and is now the Environment Minister.

As the endless unpacking and repacking of its name implies, DEFRA has suffered for many years with a florid case of organisational personality disorder. In addition to dealing with food and the environment, at various times it has or has not been in charge of dog fouling, potato classification and rules governing the quarantining of pet ferrets. It doesn't have fisheries in its name any more, but still looks after them. It did once have a role in setting food standards, but now doesn't. Sometimes it's meant to think up some sort of governmental response to climate change, and sometimes it isn't. Its current list of responsibilities also includes a random litter-pick of policy areas from eliminating Japanese knotweed to the regulation of Scotch whisky. Farmers themselves circumvent all shifts in departmental fashion by calling it 'the Ministry', a name which manages simultaneously to convey a sense of menace, longevity and ridicule, and which thus perfectly describes its status among those whom it is intended to serve.

As Whyte points out, these alterations to DEFRA's job title mean that 'there is no one single coherent vision or mission to the place'. However productive or unhealthy the working environment in other departments and however turbulent the political storms beyond the doors, there is at least the sense of a common goal. If you're at the Home Office, your mission is evidently to protect the British public. If you're at Transport, then you keep the country moving. If you're at Defence then you're there to defend, and at Education you're there to educate.

'Departments may bicker and think each other is rubbish,' Whyte told me, 'but they know together what their purpose is. In Health and Justice, the mission is so extraordinarily clear, it's beautiful. In DEFRA, I really didn't know. One morning I'd wake up and think, 'Am I here to save the world? Or am I here to kill animals? Which one is it today?''

Which, according to Whyte, means each minister has 'a massive choice of what to put their stamp on. So you have hundreds of very small, niche, specific policy areas, and rather than a big lump coming together like, say, counter-terrorism or policing, they all just shot up into one person, the Secretary of State. And it very much depends on the nature and outlook of that person as to which one of these is going to get prioritised and turned into specific action.'

So what you're saying is, it's all over the shop?

'It's an absolute rag-bag.'

As part of his attempt to mitigate his existential dilemmas Whyte spent much of his time trying to get all the various different thoughts to cohere into one single mission. 'We did try and get DEFRA to think of itself as an economic department. Huge chunks of the economy were supported and regulated by us, everything from the water industry to fisheries, agriculture, food – the biggest manufacturing sectors in the entire economy.'

Which was difficult, because he arrived under a Labour government, continued through the Conservative/Lib Dem coalition and ended with a Tory administration. Even the most resilient organisation would struggle to maintain a clear trajectory over four changes of leadership and three changes of party in ten years, let alone a government department.

It was also further complicated by the fact that, in Whitehall, DEFRA bears much of the same status as its core constituency. Since negotiating with farmers is unofficially regarded as the political equivalent of waterboarding, a posting to DEFRA can be used by prime ministers as a form of professional purgatory, a mud-lined anteroom in which erring colleagues can be left to think on their sins before being either resurrected or (professionally speaking) defenestrated. Nick Brown, the Labour Minister in charge of the foot-and-mouth outbreak of 2001, was only at MAFF because he was regarded by one faction (Blairite) as too close to the other (Brownite). More recently Michael Gove was given the post as a form of arm's-length political rehab after disgracing himself by unsuccessfully running for PM. In ministerial terms it's a godless job – no status, involves looking concerned while wearing a hairnet. Which means that, for every one minister who really does care about upland hill payments or trawlers' by-catch, there are probably three or four who would prefer to be interfering with higher education or striding down the deck of an aircraft carrier, and who thus energetically resent being stuck in meetings discussing monkfish.

But while ministerial turnover was brisk, the turnover of staff was slow. Many individuals had been at the department for a long time, and had over many years fenced out their own private fiefdoms. Which in turn meant they had very probably long ago repurposed the Civil Service code of conduct.

So you had people within the department who were working on their own agendas?

'Yes, and may have been for their whole career, twenty or thirty years.'

It sounds like herding cats.

'Yes.' He laughs, and keeps laughing. 'Yes. Intransigent, passionate cats.'

Is that different to other departments?

'Yes. Other departments have it, but nothing in that shape.'

So you could get someone whose life's work was some aspect of climate change ...?

'Yes. And then Owen Paterson (Secretary of State between 2012 and 2014) comes in and says "I don't believe in climate change." And they're like, "The world's just dropped from beneath my feet, how on earth do I work for this nutter?" It's very unprofessional, very unprofessional.'

You must have spent a lot of time managing the mental health of your staff.

'Yes.' Dry. 'And the Cabinet Minister.'

Right. So the department didn't know what it was there for. Did farmers?

'Er ... I'm not sure they really cared.'

And did they think of it as friend or enemy?

'Mostly, historically throughout the Blair government, as an enemy ... That was the getting-it thing – they saw the Labour government as very urban-based and all the officials there as very cosmopolitan, very metropolitan, didn't really understand it, didn't get it.'

Not that any of this is a new thing. Broadly speaking, farming has historically been more suspicious of Labour governments (perceived as prone to class-based grudges against time-honoured country practices, e.g. hunting, shooting) than Conservative ones (established the time-honoured country practices). Rightly or wrongly Labour is considered more likely to listen to the environmental agenda, Tories to the agricultural one. Added to which each separate set of priorities may well be posed in opposition to another. From the National Trust to the Ramblers' Association, the Royal Society for the Protection of Birds and the Country Land and Business Association there are plenty of other groups with a noisy interest in the shape of the British landscape. All are powerful, well-funded and persuasive, and all often take a very different stance on bTB or neonicotinoids to the one taken by the NFU.

And then of course there was Europe. Legislatively speaking, no one, not even the Civil Service, fully understood exactly where Europe ended and Britain began. Generally, provisional legislation on, say, the conditions governing organic barley production would be drafted in Brussels, acquire a light top-dressing of footnotes, addendums, provisos, exemptions and fudges while in committee there, make its stately way over to London, spend a couple more years gaining a further mulch of caveats, appendices, rules, consultations and by-laws somewhere in the dungeons of Smith Square and finally to be unveiled to a bated public via the DEFRA website.

If the legislation was linked to a payment, the farmer would not receive that payment without conforming to both the original EU conditions and the additional DEFRA ones. Even when the legislation was not directly linked, cross-compliance rules stipulate that farmers would be eligible to receive the money only if they had also fulfilled all Statutory Management Requirements and were thus, bureaucratically speaking, pronounced clean and free of sin. Those who had fallen from the footpath of righteousness would have penalties imposed, usually in the form of reductions to their Basic Payment Scheme (BPS). In other words, if you as a dairy farmer receiving the BPS have not calculated the amount of nitrate your cows are producing, prepared an annual four-step nitrogen plan application, proved that you have prevented soil run-off from your fields, spread exactly the right amount of manure as long as it's nowhere near a watercourse and done between April and October, and ensured that you have not destroyed any birds, trees or vegetation designated as Special Interest Features, then your payment will either be docked at source or you will be lavishly fined.

In general, farmers do not like this never-ending fall of

paper. Most recognise the sense of much of it – the banning of certain pesticides, the attempts to mitigate flooding or pollution – but almost every individual, from the largest agribusiness to the smallest holding, will at some point say, 'I didn't come into farming to fill in forms.' What tends to be resented is not the fact of oversight but DEFRA's indifference to its broader impacts. Each of those individual experts within the department naturally believed that their particular field (restoring chalk streams, air pollution, village green preservation) required regulation, and that those regulations should very likely take precedence over all other regulations. Fines would often be set immediately for any farm late or non-compliant, making a bad financial situation worse. From the sender's end (the Ministry) there could justifiably be said to be a tidy proven outfall of work going out to the wider world. From the farmer's end it often felt like an incoherent deluge of sanctions, instructions, verbiage and countermands, each form insisting on its own life-stopping importance and every meaning-free demand sludging up their inbox.

On a day-to-day level the majority of farmers grumble and comply. The inspections become just something which goes with the job. Even so, the gulf in understanding between urban drafters and rural enactors does sometimes become apparent. A few years ago DEFRA announced that all its forms were henceforth to be filed online, a directive which makes perfect sense in Central London where broadband coverage is universal, but which works less well in the lands that time and BT forgot, including the distant hill farms which the payment schemes are most intended to support.

More generally, there is also a sense that agricultural policy is not a constant head-down march in one steady direction, but something whimsical and vague which skips off in a different direction every time the department gets a new minister.

In among the rising or falling hemlines of butter mountains, set-aside, dairy quotas, crop diversification, being nice to birds or bees, being nice to trees, being nice to mussels or hedges, is a general sense that, like diesel and roughage, the regulatory must-haves of one year may very well become the discards of another. One decade it's all about increasing yield, the next it's all about welfare. After the war, agricultural policy was designed to ensure we could never starve again. Then it was designed to make us competitive both in Europe and globally. Now, who knows?

The traditional government rejoinder is to point out that there's no such thing as free money, and that any farmer wanting anything off the taxpayer should legitimately be expected to account for it. They also point to the achievements of the system. Greater regulation has ensured the return of many birds of prey, ensured far better animal welfare standards and vastly improved both the traceability of British foods and their value. Because of regulation Britain still has fish in its rivers and bats in its attics. Regulation has kept out disease and kept in quality. Or, if we were to look at it another way, if it wasn't for DEFRA and its bureaucratic ancestors, we'd all still be eating horses and strewing our rivers with sodium cyanide. We'd have fished our seas dry, grubbed up all our hedgerows and modified our crops past the point of recognition. Regulation may have a bad name, but just try the alternative.

They also point out that farming profits from government largesse. At present there are still grants – not loans, but real giveaway money – for everything from the coverings for slurry tanks to the concreting of yards. At present, there's money for planting a tree and pounds by the metre for laying a hedge, hundreds for a ground source heat pump and thousands for biomass. There's money for putting in forestry tracks and money for the machinery to get there. It may not be there forever and there may be many strings attached, but still, it seems a bit rich (in all senses) to complain on the one hand while banking the cheque on the other.

Nevertheless, the hum of discontent does occasionally reach a pitch loud enough to prompt a governmental response. Traditionally this response takes the form of a long inquiry followed by a long document with several further regulatory recommendations. A good example is DEFRA's answer to agricultural bureaucracy and paperwork. Since 2000 there have been several working groups and task forces on reducing red tape within farming, including the Curry Report of 2002, the Hampton Review of 2005 and the EU's Better Regulation Commission. Some of those have been looking at one sector such as animal health, while others promise sweeping changes and come with thrusty, alliterative mission statements: 'Reducing Burdens, Improving Outcomes', 'Risk, Responsibility and Regulation – Whose Risk Is It Anyway?'

Collectively both the EU and the DEFRA bureaucratic reviews have themselves generated an impressive quantity of paper and bureaucracy. The most recent and specific was the 2011 Independent Farming Regulation Task Force Report chaired by Richard Macdonald, which ran to 152 pages plus appendices containing a further 215 recommendations. It characterised the farming view of inspections – and by extension much of the regulatory framework – as 'intrusive, time-consuming, heavy-handed, burdensome, unsympathetic, uninformed about farm-business practice, and intended to catch them out'. At the back of the report was a list of the paperwork required of one 'typical large horticultural business'. The list ran to five densely filled pages, and included everything from HSE COSHH assessments to agricultural waste exemption forms, glasshouse glass repair records, procedural accountability logs, metal detector check forms, field staff hygiene requirements letters and the toilet cleaning log. Macdonald recommended a lighter touch. So far, almost none of the report's recommendations have been implemented.

In 2015, the then Business Secretary Sajid Javid ordered a further review of red tape within several departments, including DEFRA. And in 2018 Dame Glenys Stacey published her report into farming regulation. Broadly speaking, all the reports – Curry, Hampton, Macdonald and Stacey – have come to similar conclusions: the current system is inflexible, punitive, contradictory and in many cases unenforceable. There's a lack of communication between the five different branches of DEFRA responsible for oversight and a lack of trust between the inspectors and the inspected. Sometimes regulations had done good – protected wildlife, preserved a particular area from contamination, provided a better understanding of bTB's prevalence – but often, it seemed based on suspicion. No wonder farmers were not enthusiastic: a further National Audit Office Report in 2012 had pointed out that complying with regulations cost each farm an average of a tenth of its annual profit. At that time farm inspections, disease surveillance and compliance tests were costing the country £47 million a year.

Still, says Whyte, adding a final disclaimer, it's not like DEFRA can really do anything.

'As a civil servant I can tell you we don't do much, but [farmers are] constantly looking to government, they'll criticise every word. As much as I loved them, the bovine TB strategy, the dependency on the government to get that done … well, please be really careful about this, but a bunch of us had to spend two summers down in the fucking West Country to help get those culls off the ground. Because they [farmers] were like, "Why don't we just get a box of cartridges …?" It was like, "No!" It was tough on everyone, but they've got to get more self-reliant.'

On the other hand, dealing with recalcitrant farmers did at least get him out of the office. Which is probably more than most of his colleagues. 'The vast majority of DEFRA staff have never lived in or had anything to do with the countryside. They just don't get it.'

So leaving aside farming itself, what proportion of DEFRA staff come from a rural background?

'Tiny. Tiny.'

Apart from a shared lack of fondness for life beyond London, the only thing which does apparently unite everyone at the department is a shared lack of fondness for the agricultural payments system.

'Every single one of them would love to have got rid of the subsidies and the bureaucracy that went with them. The Tories are no friends of subsidy. Maybe one or two of them who had been farmers find it hard to kick, but they knew the politics, they knew the European dimension, they knew they couldn't do it. But they would have loved to have liberated farming, and to a lesser extent fisheries, from the weird dysfunctional reliance that subsidies cause.'

And yet the payments remain. 'The reason that even the most gung-ho free-market Tory wouldn't ever remove the subsidies in one go is because they'd have a massive competitive disadvantage overnight, because all their serious global competitors have subsidies as well. So either everyone does it, or no one does it.'

Whyte stops for a second, thinks, and swings the whole thing tidily to an end. 'It makes Justice look like a doddle.'

9

Cropped

There's an old man moving among the trees in the fielded backlands near the Wye, tracking slowly down the rows through the sleet and wet sun. There's a rainbow in the sky behind him and as he stoops and rises, the light sparks up through the rain and crowns him with a halo against the grey-green outlines of the branches.

The trees stand with a strip of grass laid between them, with the loose weeds round their trunks round-upped into submission. Though there are three different varieties of cider apple in this field, the aim is to produce a tree shaped in profile like the point of an arrow and ranked next to its near-identical neighbour. At the base, the trunks of each are clean and free of snags. Since any low branches would be damaged by the mechanical harvesters, the trick is to nip them off below the knees and to clip away any shoots trying to sneak skyward. There's no more than about a metre side-to-side between each tree, which means that over the years they have gradually espaliered themselves, folding together to form spiny green walls. Each one has been planted so exactly that as the liquid afternoon light falls through them it's like standing in a fractal, a multiplying field of lines running in perfect geometrics over the land.

Left to their own devices none of these trees would look like this. A wild apple tree is outspread, a thin-heeled stem tippling below a party of limbs flung out over the ground, its canopy as shagged as a Seventies demi-wave. It takes up space, fires up new branches, flings out cheerleading pom-poms of mistletoe. It's prolific, disorderly, lichened with age or shooting with youth. The trees here are instead the product of many decades of tidying for mechanisation, a forest without wildness, every tree accounted and understood. The effect, oddly enough, is disorienting: you could be lost here among the anonymous vanishing points, one row as clean as another, each field offering the same thing in the same way.

It's bare winter now and, apart from the far-off grunt of a truck, there's nobody around but David Newport. At every tree he pauses, examines it for signs of disorder, and then slices it into shape. There's a patience to this, and – at its best – a rhythm to reading a tree. It's also a job requiring only the most basic tools: thick leather gloves, a pair of secateurs, a ruthless pruning saw. David has a tractor as a base station and a packed lunch (four sandwiches, banana, Thermos of coffee, six Jacob's Cream Crackers with cheese) which has remained the same for so long that his wife once wrote to Jacob's suggesting that perhaps forty-five years of undeviating cracker loyalty qualified David for some kind of biscuit-related reward programme.

For four months a year every year this is his work, day in, day out: trees, weather, sick or healthy wood, the shape of the past and of things to come. In all, he calculates, he does maybe two, two and a half rows a day, which, if there's roughly a hundred trees per row and maybe 45 acres of this particular variety, 40 of another, makes it … crikey – he pauses, thinks – never actually totted it up, but call it 12,000 trees over the whole season? Once in a while someone turns up wanting work experience or training, but generally it's just him, a pocketful of BBC radio, and the intermittent clip of the loppers.

He doesn't particularly mind the solitary nature of his work. 'I enjoy it when there's someone around to help. But it takes a while to teach them what to do. Some pick it up quickly, and some don't get it. It depends on them – sometimes it's people who are very chatty and sometimes they don't like to talk. But I'm used to being out there, and I'm just as happy alone. I shouldn't think like that, but I get set in my ways, especially after a long time of working on my own.'

He'll work through all conditions, he explains. If it's cold he'll carry on, and if it's more cold (say minus six or so) he'll carry on, and if he's soaked through he'll carry on, and if it's blowing a gale he'll carry on, and if it's getting dark he'll carry on. As long as he can actually reach work, he'll keep going, through snow, ice and national hysterics. He remains indifferent to storms, named or otherwise, and the only trouble with heatwaves is having to wear those boil-in-the-bag overtrousers. The only things which stop David are too much snow blown against the branches, and a double-glove rainfall – i.e., if it's so wet he's soaked through two pairs of thick leather gloves. A genuine rain-proof all-weather pro.

A lifetime's weather has marked him. He has a broad, flat face, a smile of absolute candour, and the most wolfishly white-blue eyes I've ever seen – crazy-dog pale, though warmed by steadiness and toleration. He makes his arrival into this line of work sound easy and coincidental, a thing of mild surprise, but in fact David is a rarity. He came into this through the old traditional route, a path which has itself now vanished into the undergrowth. Born in Kent, he started working aged sixteen in the dessert apple orchards there, discovering how to plant and tend the best eating or cooking varieties. It wasn't that he particularly wanted to work outside, he says, but it was a job, it paid reasonable money, and there was satisfaction in the seasonal rhythm of pruning, planting, grafting, spraying, harvesting and then reverting back to pruning again. He got his craftsman's qualification in soft-fruit horticulture and, after several years moving around the apple-growing counties of England, began working for a big fruit nursery in Hampshire. It was a post which brought with it a tied cottage and job security. It also gave him experience with most of the fruits which can be grown in the UK. Nine years on, he and the family moved over to a cooperative farm in Herefordshire working with both dessert and cider varieties, before transferring to Lulham.

All those decades of experience have given David a width and flex of skill that few can match. It also makes him very hard to emulate. No one else, certainly no one else with anything like his level of expertise, will take the job. David is now sixty-two and thinking about retirement, but though the farm has been looking for someone to train first as his assistant and then as his replacement for the last six years, either it gets one or two applicants who vanish once they realise what the work entails, or it gets none at all.

'People aren't so hardy now,' says David. 'If it was just tractor work they could probably fill the position easy, but it's not. People like the machinery, but the more physical side, they're not interested in it – the next generation just hasn't had to do any physical work – but if they tried it, they might get into it.'

'If Dave wasn't here, could I do Dave's job?' the farm's owner George Snell asks himself. 'No chance. I wouldn't want to do it.'

So what are you going to do when David goes?

'I really don't know,' admits Will Jackson, his manager. 'Hope he stays, I guess.'

In other words, they hope they know David well enough to know that he'll last about a week in retirement before getting restless. 'I'll enjoy it for about three days,' he says, 'and then I expect I'll start making a real nuisance of myself.'

To an outsider there seems something everlasting about David's job – all that vigorous, rosy-cheeked seasonality, all that cider and apple blossom. Trees are trees, after all. They don't move and, since it takes a while for them to grow to maturity, then surely they can't be as vulnerable to the same winds of agricultural change as lambs or wheat?

Herefordshire is one of the four apple-growing counties in the UK (the others being Kent, Worcestershire and Somerset), and thus one of Britain's main producers of cider. Since cider apples are a different variety to eating, or dessert, apples, most of the orchards here are on contract to an international brewing company whose farmers produce around a third of the supply grown in the UK. Approximately 100,000 tonnes are produced in the various county orchards contracted to the company, but it has recently been running down or trying to extricate itself from many of its contracts. A few years ago the company took a bet that the UK market for cider would get larger. It drew up more contracts and encouraged its existing farmers to plant more trees. As it turned out, it was right about the expansion in cider drinking, but wrong about the consequences. Other large brewery companies had made a similar calculation and, from a stable situation in which there were only one or two big players, suddenly there were lots – not just importers like Carlsberg and Magners, but small local microbreweries making popular craft ciders, all of whom began to gnaw away at the company's market share. As things stand it has kept its position, but it's only holding steady, not expanding. Which in turn means that many of those orchards (both ancient and modern) are now being grubbed up, acre after acre felled and piled in a corner, 20,000 potential apples flat-packed for firewood.

On a flickery day in mid-December I arrived at Lower Lulham to do a day's tree-pruning with David. Several men in sturdy boots, check shirts and high-vis were sitting at desks in a converted chicken shed, the closest of whom was a tall fifty-something blond man with a worn smile and an unstated but evident air of command: George Snell. He asked me what I was here for and, when I explained, took me into the boardroom and pointed to a row of photographs on one wall.

The photographs were all aerial shots of the farm, starting in the 1960s when recently purchased by George's father, and ending a couple of years ago. When Hugh Snell bought the farm in the 1950s it was a conventional mixed holding. Hugh first began growing vegetables (sprouts, potatoes, cabbage), and then in the 1970s took on contracts to produce cider apples for Bulmers and blackcurrants for Ribena. After a while he expanded into poultry production and then went sideways, first into poplar planting and then into wider forestry. Shifting, protean, mutable – the Snells' sense for business was all that the land itself (fixed, solid, grounding) is not. They got rid of the poultry, changed up into timber, expanded the Bulmers contract, planted some trees, grubbed up others. At the moment it's the wood business that is doing best. Lower Lulham is now the UK's largest supplier of kiln-dried hardwood logs, and the fruit is just an adjunct to that. George and his brother Nick have taken the resources they have (a smallholding of good land) and sculpted it into something which doesn't just support them and their families, but a further thirty employees.

The proof of all the changes is inscribed into the architecture. The first photo shows the farm as it must have been in the eighteenth century – a red-brick house surrounded by a cluster of stables and byres. There's a garden and a pond and a little patch of willow trees, and somewhere in the faded Kodachrome colours is a sense of a new world already pulling against the old. The next few show a rubbly muddle where one of the brick byres had been and the beginnings of two large poultry sheds, one of which we're now sitting in. By the 1980s the pond had been moved to the back of the house, and in its place were the white-roofed beginnings of the log business. There's also an outdoor riding arena and the low corridor shapes of stables. The most recent photograph shows the farm as it is now: a log-pile with a caravan site attached. Four vast steel sheds fill the landscape, and round the edges of the tracks are dun-coloured mountains of wood. The farmhouse itself is now almost the smallest of the buildings there.

As with many other businesses it has been the move out of conventional stock or arable farming which has, ironically enough, ensured Lulham's survival. The Snells weren't alone in recognising the value of diversification. Back in the 1970s and 1980s, add-on businesses were fairly straightforward: B&Bs, holiday lets, direct sales, pick-your-own, shooting, livery stables, renting out empty buildings. Now, diversification has diversified, becoming a way either of keeping afloat when times are hard or of creating a direct bridge between those who grow the food and those who consume it. In the twenty-first century, schemes have included everything from the obviously related – microbreweries, alpacas, forestry – to windfarms, motorway service stations and papermills. The Glastonbury music festival and many of its younger offspring are just very successful forms of farm diversification. Almost half of all British holdings now have some form of enterprise or income drawing on the assets (human or otherwise) of the core, which means that farmers often find themselves learning a lot of completely unrelated skills in order to be able to continue with the original one. It also means that someone who might be good with beef cattle or seed genetics ends up also having to be good with the economics of tidal energy, or at reviving overdosed musos.

Collectively, the Snells have taken a gamble on the future of farming being very big, and very clever. George Snell says repeatedly he thinks of himself as a businessman, not a farmer. 'The farming's not important – it's just a means to an end now. I just see the land as an opportunity, and it's the business keeps me going. The wood business, the horse business, the things I really enjoy.'

Which doesn't mean he feels no obligation to the land. 'There's some connection with the land and the way things are done. You can't learn it, really. It's here, really' – he thumps his chest – 'isn't it?'

A few miles away on the other side of the county, his elder brother Anthony has done the same thing in a different way. Like George he has taken a smallholding of land, wrenched it away from convention and worked it as hard as he could. He and his wife Christine now run one of the largest soft-fruit businesses in the UK, supplying Tesco, Sainsbury's and M&S with raspberries, strawberries and blackcurrants. Back in the 1980s they bought 150 acres of land near Ross-on-Wye and, after being unable to make a profit farming it traditionally (beef, sheep), they diversified first into salad crops and then into fruit. As with Lulham, their landholding isn't huge. They own 200 acres but rent a further 250. If Lulham is mostly logs, then the land at Harewood End is now mainly plastic. Look down the clefts of the hill in summer and the fields are ridged white with the curved profiles of polytunnels, beneath which row after row of patent strawberries dangle like Christmas garlands off chest-height drainage trays. Over on another part of the farm the raspberry bushes are big tousled things, shoots sprawling with ripe fruit, and the full punnets gleam with perfect uniform vigour. Even in mid-October lines of pickers still move in tandem down the raised rows, selecting the best fruit in a colour spectrum from postbox to alizarin.

One of the most effective ways of smoothing out the notori-
ous moodiness of the British weather is to make it irrelevant:
to bring the strawberry plants under cover so they live under
plastic or glass or below low-energy lamps. In here, there need
be no rain or sun or snow, no slipping through thickening rimes
of mud or groping round an autumn fog. A whole year's crop
can't be written off by a five-minute hailstorm and no one can
overturn the tractor on an unseen patch of frost. Gales aren't
great, admittedly, and the whole system relies on a solid and
continuous supply of reasonably priced electricity, but if you
want to grow chrysanthemums in February then the consensus
now seems to be that the first thing you need is a roof over your
head. Besides, protecting the fruit here expands the growing
season at both ends of the year.

In the packhouse the fruit which has made it this far is being
sorted by a line of women dressed in warm layers, blue overall
coats and hairnets. They stand beneath the hard white lights
facing a series of laminated training guides pinned to the packhouse wall showing images of good fruit and bad – strawberries
with neck-split or powdery mildew, immature raspberries with
sooty shoulders. The women sort and pack patiently, filling the
blue crates until a supervisor comes to remove the work they've
done so far.

Opposite them is another line on which the completed
punnets are covered and labelled, and behind that is a stack of
new packing crates for supermarket deliveries, conspicuously
decorated with Union Jacks. Though it's late in the season and
the packhouse is at minimum capacity, this is a sophisticated
and intricate operation. The machinery, the polytunnels, the
trays, the plants, the staff – all of this has taken huge calculation
and investment. In addition to the full-time staff, all soft-fruit
farms employ seasonal workers. Many of the tasks which
would once have been done by hand – cutting hay or corn,

storing grain – are now done by machine. Apples and pears can be mechanically harvested, but soft fruit can still only be hand-picked, an anomaly which producers would dearly love to roboticise but which for the moment remains a human task.

And the work is controversial partly because, among many farmers, there is thought to be a bias away from British workers. One large West Country fruit farmer cites a year when they had to advertise in the UK for pickers. They got 400 applicants, 100 went to interview, 50 were offered work, but at the end of two weeks only one was still there. 'The harsh reality is that it's not even worth trying with British people – the younger generation just wouldn't last,' he says. 'Though, to be fair, neither would the younger generation of Eastern Europeans.' It remains to be seen whether Covid-19 and the subsequent recession will change this, but the current crop of pickers, thrown out of jobs in cafés or shops, may well prove to be more tenacious. They also tell a very different tale to the one told by the managers.

Many farms have relied for years on an entire village coming over every year during the season to pick, families of different ages living in static caravans on site and working in shifts. They pick with the efficiency of many years' practice and, while they're there, have few expenses other than rent, food and drink. British workers, on the other hand, have to travel from home, which often means that their earnings don't even cover their transport costs. On some farms, workers won't be told until the end of one day if they will be needed the next, and all of them may be expected to go home after a couple of hours if nothing is ready to pick. And on some farms the financial goalposts tend to wander. If workers are earning too much on an hourly rate then they'll be shifted to piecework, and if they're too productive on piecework they'll be shifted back to hours. There is no security, not much training and usually only the exhortation to pick more, better, faster.

In the case of both Lower Lulham and Harewood End, the original farm has been almost entirely subsumed by the new businesses. The fruit or the wood has made possible both the end of an old form of farming and a flourishing of the new, and the rewards for that are huge, agile, rich businesses. The price is a lot of sleepless nights.

A hundred miles away over in Somerset Bert's daughter Sarah and son-in-law Rob Keelan have taken the same gamble with a different product. Back in the 1940s Long Acre was a 340-acre mixed stock farm, but when two neighbouring farms came up for sale in the 1950s and 1960s Rob's grandfather went to the bank, asked for a loan on the security of the land and bought both. When the time came to inherit, Rob's father, Ellis Keelan, bought out his siblings and kept doing the same. Now Long Acre is 1,800 acres. Of those 450 are potatoes and the rest are divided between arable, energy crops and poultry units. The mainstay of the farm business are the 470,000 chickens Rob rears on a forty-eight-day cycle for Tesco and McDonald's. Over here everything is bigger – the sums are bigger, the sheds are bigger, the machinery is bigger, the debt is bigger. Long Acre is doing well, but it's doing well on low interest rates and an £8 million loan.

Rob Keelan is a welcoming presence with a tussock of gingerish hair and a broad, open face. He and his father play rugby, and it shows – both men are big enough to stop a combine, though in character Rob is gentler and more considered than Ellis, who generally gets through life on stress and a short fuse.

'I never really mention my divorce,' said Ellis, though on the few occasions I've met him the divorce has made its appearance early, and hard. It wasn't so much the dent to his pride, though that was significant. It was that the settlement had forced him to sell land. Nothing, not rugby losses, not bad yields, not the cancellation of a big contract, could have hurt more.

The Keelans' methods may be controversial (they get through a lot of chickens) but, after three hours roaming around every topic in agriculture – Renewable Heat Incentive (RHI) tariffs, Brexit, AI technology, sheep husbandry, world population statistics, solar PV kilowatt hourly returns, nitrogen inputs, inheritance tax reliefs, cattle prices, poultry welfare, projected grain prices in the American Midwest, planning infrastructure, systemic pesticide legislation, traceability, supermarket economics, cats, dogs, snow, children – I had yet to find a topic on which both of them couldn't give an informed and eloquent view. Some of it came with top-spin, but all of it was thoughtful, in-depth, backed up with figures, and based on long hands-on knowledge.

As with most farmers the Keelans' requirements are entirely specific. At the moment they produce chickens and chips. In physical terms chickens don't need much at all – just space for a shed and several hundred thousand pounds' worth of resources. Potatoes, on the other hand, are easy to grow but greedy on the soil and prone to blight. The Keelans put a lot of care into building and replenishing their soils but, even with plenty of extra organic matter, potatoes have to be grown one year on, seven years off. They need the richest, cleanest, most productive land – best of all if it's land that's never been used for spuds before. Potatoes take a lot of nutrients out, and must be sown in a fine tilth: soil that's been ploughed and sifted to the softness of breadcrumbs. Constant rain early in the season clogs that soil, rotting the seed and gluing a slick black mulch to everything it comes into contact with. In autumn any mechanical attempt to harvest the remaining crop either gets bogged down or bruises it so badly shaking the clots off that the crop becomes inedible anyway. When the tractors and harvesters leave the fields they drag mud onto the roads and then everyone complains it's filthy and dangerous. To lift potatoes requires at least two tractors, one towing the harvester and the other towing the trailer, both travelling down the field in tandem with a relay of trailers filling up and returning. The harvester breaks down, the trailer gets stuck, someone needs more oil, it gets dark, the lights fail, it starts to rain. When it rains heavily the water begins to collect around the edges of the field, sauntering at first, then leaping in a brown river down the slope before wheeling sideways from the gate and along the lane beyond, taking a couple of hundred earth years with it. Stand on a hill during a deluge and you can watch what looks like half a field flood straight out the county.

In December 2012 it rained almost without ceasing. Half the Keelans' potatoes dissolved where they lay and much of the rest rotted in the boxes. At that point they were contracted for 6,500 tons a year, but could get only 3,300 tons into the shed. Technically that represented a breach of contract, and McCain, one of the companies Long Acre supplies, could have forced the Keelans to buy themselves out. As it was, Britain had such a shortfall of potatoes that McCain honoured the contract and took what it could. The Keelans survived but made a loss of £600,000 that year. The NFU later calculated that over £600 million of wheat and potatoes had simply slipped back into the ground.

'I was a casual smoker at the time,' says Rob, 'but I wasn't very casual about trying to get potatoes out of the ground. I used to drive the pick-up to the gate of the field and watch tractors get stuck while chain-smoking.'

Once out of the field and back on the farm the potatoes get tipped from the trailer into the grader, a raised conveyor with two rotating belts in between which five people stand, lifting out stones or damaged potatoes as they arrive and chucking them into the two bins beside them. The potatoes are sorted before sliding onto another section which grades them according to size and then drops them into different boxes. It's not hard work but it is relentless – the belt moves steadily from left to right, fast enough to keep its speed but slow enough to spot and remove the rejects. You have to get your eye in, but once you do the job could become something almost somnambulant, a hand-tranced task done while half elsewhere. Because the work is seasonal, each farm has its own arrangements. Some put out the call every autumn and get a mixture of regular graders and one-offs. The work and the workers are carefully scrutinised, but there are plenty who appear, work hard for a couple of months and then vanish. Other farms work on an established relationship with one particular area – some villages in Estonia or Lithuania send over a whole team of graders year after year for the duration of the season.

The physical practicalities of harvesting aren't the only consideration – the spuds' taste and appearance also play a part. Over the decades Ellis has been through several different types: King Edward ('very difficult to grow'), Romano ('looked beautiful, tasted like shit'), Penta ('deep eyes – couldn't peel 'em'), and now Pentland Dell. One year Ellis ended up with a lot of unwanted Pentas. 'They left them on my farm once, a thousand tons. I couldn't sell them. They made me grow them, then they found out, "Well, what we done that for?" And they didn't buy them off me, though it was contracted. They just said the skins weren't good enough. I lost a hundred grand one year just on that.'

A pause. Like most people I have not seen a thousand tons of dumped potatoes. I haven't seen a parsnip mountain, or a carrot hillock, or a lettuce summit. I've only seen a lorryload of cider apples rejected by the processor (too small, too dirty, too late, too green, problem with the rota, problem with the machines, operator off sick) and left to rot in a field. That was about four tons – nothing, really, in the scale of things. But just as with Andersons, it turns out there's a big difference between knowing something happens and actually staring right at it – the size, the scale, the time it took for these plants to draw the heat and the rain of a particular summer, to swell with quiet splendour and then to end up oozing down the bucket of a digger before being loaded back into the earth. Potatoes and apples are not animals, and this is not killing bull calves. But those mounds of edible produce leave behind them an unease.

Still. The spuds that the Keelans grow are not cooking potatoes which might be rejected by the consumer because they don't look right. McCain doesn't need its potatoes to bake or roast or mash, or to look great on a plate next to a Sunday roast. It just needs to ensure that they fry well and that it can get the maximum number of long rectangular plank-shaped things out of a short round wonky-shaped thing. Thus the company can and will reject what the Keelans grow if the dry matter is over or under a certain amount, if there's more than 15 per cent defects – including 'mechanical defects' – if there's brown centres, irregularities (i.e., the potato isn't potato-shaped enough), natural cracks, bacterial infection, blight, worms, slugs, wet rot, dry rot, gangrene, skin spot, frost, silver scurf and hollow heart. Then there is the time limit. If potatoes are kept for too long the starch turns to sugar, meaning that the 'fry colour' is wrong – in other words, when they're fried or grilled they come up black. Nobody wants a black chip. Unsurprisingly, the economics and the complexities of growing potatoes have pushed many farmers out of the market. There used to be 300,000 UK farmers doing this in the 1980s. Now there are around 2,000. Even many of the big growers got out because the stress and the sums were so great.

The other half of the Keelans' crop is also indoors. In the past decade or so the British appetite for beef, lamb and pork has stayed steady or declined, but our love of chicken as a light not-quite-meat has increased. The Keelans grow theirs on a forty-eight-day cycle, meaning they get from chick to slaughtered bird over a forty-eight-day rotation. The aim is to produce a healthy, tasty, well-bred bird, free from disease and reared to their suppliers' welfare standards. But more than that, the imperative is to give the public what they want – not what they say they want, but what they actually want. As Rob points out, if you ask a hundred people on their way into a supermarket what they think of poultry production, the majority will say they're all in favour of free-range, organic, £8 corn-fed happy hens. If, when those same individuals emerge from the supermarket a while later, you have a look at what's in their bags it's the ordinary £4 chicken, the 3-for-2 version, no make-up, no fancy nails. In the Keelans' opinion it's cost, always cost, which drives the British consumer's choices. Which is why they don't just rear one single standard bird but several different types: a family bird (feeds four), a meal-for-one bird, a mid-week special and a Sunday lunch. The birds are fed according to the weight they're designed to reach when finished – a range of live-sizes from XS to XXXL.

A few months later at Open Farm Sunday, Tesco and McDonald's have rolled out the interpretation boards, and squads of double-muscled blondes are offering tours of the larger combines. Rob is around but Ellis is nowhere to be seen. Instead one of the senior managers at Avara, one of the UK's largest food businesses, is acting as gatekeeper. Talking to him by a table full of children ('Hello there! Can you tell me where bread comes from?'), I notice that he refers to Long Acre as 'our' farm and the Keelans as 'our' farmers. As do the various representatives from Tesco, McCain and McDonald's. Yes, this is our farm, he says, but it's one among many spread out all over the country.

Among its other divisions, Avara is a major poultry processor with facilities all over the country slaughtering and packing chicken, turkey and duck. In 2013 nearly 95 per cent of the UK population ate white meat and most did so frequently – at least twice a week. Over the past few years, our taste for it has flourished. In December 2012, 65.5 million 'broilers' (any chicken raised for consumption) were slaughtered in the UK; by the same month in 2019, that had risen to 104.5 million. Break that down into parts, and in the first part of 2020 when lockdown began, an average of just over 20 million chickens were being slaughtered every seven days. Many of those came from, and through, Avara. And, as an international conglomerate with holdings all over the world, its job is to ensure choice and consistency. So if a retailer orders so many birds per week, it knows it is guaranteed to receive those birds on time and to standard. Which means it and the Keelans and all their other farmers remain in an everlasting tangle with the laws of nature. Living things die of unspecified causes, or get diseases, or overheat, or get too big, or grow too slowly. Nature races or falters, mutates, twists out from under our control. And still every day we want milk (the same milk) in our coffee and chicken drumsticks (the same drumsticks) for tea. To produce a standard product from a streamlined management of a natural process is, says the senior manager, 'a challenge'. He himself, meanwhile, has a nice old-fashioned smallholding not so far away.

And so these rough curves of Somerset are now edged with the low, flat profiles of poultry sheds, all lines and right angles, and – when the wind is turned – a raw, ammoniac reek. In addition to the six sheds at Long Acre the Keelans still have several hundred acres of arable land on which they grow corn to feed the birds. Those chickens create muck which then gets used as nitrogen-rich fertiliser back on the land. It's the same circle as a compost heap at home, but on a bigger, pushier scale. All their poultry is housed in big open spaces, free to roam around and equally free to be examined at any moment by one of their suppliers. Tesco gives only twenty minutes' notice of an inspection, and the last time Rob had one it was at 6.30 in the morning. When its inspectors arrive they cover everything from feed times to hours of darkness to access to feed and water to perches and 'environmental enrichment'. They will go through the paperwork for hours, and walk through the sheds with paper overshoes which, if tested in the lab later for traces of campylobacter or enteritis and found positive, can make the difference between the farm's continuance or permanent shut-down. As Ellis admits, he got failed a few years ago because he didn't have a complete workmen's toilet cleaning rota.

Both Rob's and Ellis's phones ring constantly. At one stage Ellis takes a call and goes out of the room. When he returns, he sits down again. 'That was a neighbouring small farmer. He wants us to buy his land. I've been putting him off and putting him off because we can't afford it. And he wants to come and meet me, and he says, "I need to know, Ellis." He wants me to buy it because we used to play football together.'

His land borders yours?

'Yes.'

How much has he got to sell?

'Thirty-eight acres. But that's half a million.'

Is it good?

'No, it's rubbish.'

Rob looks out of the window. 'It's just flat, and it's close to town.'

Well-maintained?

'No,' says Ellis. 'It's grass, it's not got subsidies ...'

Rob, derisive: 'It's got reeds on some of it.'

What are you going to tell him?

'Well, we'll have a chat.'

A look passes between them. The conversation moves on. They'll almost certainly buy it. Land is land and, as the old cliché goes, they aren't making any more of it. The soil might be bad, it'll certainly mean they have to borrow more, but who knows what its future strategic value might be? Better to take it now than turn it down and watch someone else stick a load of multimillion-pound greenhouses on it. Both father and son agree that the only way to move forward is to get larger: to amalgamate, to grow, to squeeze the economies of scale to the point where they really begin to yield.

I wonder how Rob deals with all of these competing demands. He has a young family and, between the inspections, the debt, the weather and all his other interests, I can't see how he ever gets to sleep. Like 2012 or 2019, when he couldn't harvest his potatoes – does he mind that kind of stress?

'I'm thirty-five, so no, I don't mind it. I don't want it to happen, but I'm young enough to think, "Well, you just bore on, don't you?"'

But the sums of money involved here are so much higher.

'But that's only a situation thing, isn't it? To some businesses that two-thousand-pound invoice they haven't been paid is the difference between being able to pay their mortgage or not. For us the sums may be bigger, but the importance of it is the same.'

What about the subsidy?

They get it for the corn they grow, Rob says, but they've also planned for a world beyond it. 'I've got no issue with that at all – I actually think I can farm without a subsidy. It will probably cut out any excess in the system.'

So if it was withdrawn tomorrow, what would that do to you?

'Ummm …' He pauses. 'It would obviously be a negative impact.'

What percentage of the farm's income does it represent?

Depends on the year, because, despite all the audits and all the controls, life always gets in the way. In 2017, probably about 25 per cent of their net profit. Still, neither of them believes that the subsidy will – or should – continue much longer. Rob: 'It's very difficult to argue that you should give money to farmers when people can't get an operation.'

So what does that mean for the small places like Rise Farm? Do you think they're going to survive?

Both simultaneously: 'No.'

You have to be big?

'Yes,' says Ellis. 'The big get bigger.'

'Or,' says Rob, 'they have another job.'

In Ellis's view, the big will always eat the small. The small, and probably the hobby farmers too. 'We know people who have the opportunity to farm, and they're clueless – they've been in the pub and they've been doing a photography course or whatever, and you talk to them and you think, "You ain't going to survive, mate." But you like them so you don't tell them.'

So would you trust a farmer who wasn't born into it?

Both father and son speak at once. 'Yes,' says Rob. 'No,' says Ellis.

Rob looks at his dad. 'Why not?!'

''Cause it don't exist,' says Ellis. 'They don't have the knowledge. You have to have that embedded love and knowledge of it or there's no chance.'

There follows a short, good-natured tussle – Rob reels off a couple of first-generation names, Ellis says they're few and far between, Rob says you need new blood coming into farming, Ellis says they don't last.

So what do you do? I ask. At the moment farming is closed. You've got an industry in need of new entrants, an ageing workforce, and there's plenty of farmers who think you've got no chance unless you're born to it. The only other job like this is the monarchy.

Rob laughs. 'And farmers are kings within their own little kingdoms.'

And, just as at Rise, each inheritor has to be free to take the farm into the future. As Ellis admits, it's Rob more than him who has driven the farm in this new direction. 'My dad brought up four kids on three hundred and forty acres, whereas my son couldn't do what he wants to do with his family without ... pffff, two thousand?'

Rob looks at him over the top of his coffee mug.

'This farm is worth eight million,' continues Ellis. 'I'm leaving him eight million the day I die. He'll be paying for it for the whole of his life, but if he wasn't here I wouldn't have chickens, I wouldn't have rented farms and I wouldn't have bought farms.'

'How many acres of spuds would you be growing?' says Rob.

'Hundred?' Pause. Stare. 'I'd have six hundred acres of corn. One man, a few men coming in to help, I'd have managed to pay off my divorce and I wouldn't have the stress of a massively growing business. I probably wouldn't have any FIT or any RHI, I'd have nice equipment ...'

Rob smiles. Somehow Ellis comes across as one of life's natural predators.

So do you both enjoy it?

'Farming?' says Rob. 'Yes!' For the first time, there is real zest in his voice. 'I love it! Do you know what I like most? I like driving tractors. Do you know what I do the least? Drive tractors. I spend three and a half days a week on a computer. Emails, accounts, filling out forms for this, that and the other, getting ready for the next inspection ...'

Whatever the size or scale of farm, it still needs the kit to go with it: the ploughs and harrows, the flails, sprayers, spreaders, cultivators, balers, tractors, combines, quads, chainsaws, trailers and chain harrows, the bits and bobs of assorted kit required to get crops into the ground or out of it. Livestock needs handling systems, fences, crushes, gates and races, penning systems, things built and adapted over generations to fit the buildings they compartmentalise, things to lift or feed or scrape, objects designed to control, enclose or direct. And farmers need machines to help with the heavy lifting: telehandlers and cherry pickers, dumpers and pick-ups. Everything is bigger than it used to be. A small rectangular haybale weighs around 25 kg, a single round bale around 200 kg. The kit needs updating, upgrading; it falls apart, needs maintenance, can't be repaired, they no longer make the parts.

Some farmers make a fetish of the engines themselves – £200,000 tractors, half a million in harvesters – while others like to ensure their machinery is colour coordinated. Those who make the accessories can now tone them to the same shade as a farmer's Fendt crop sprayer or Kubota RTV. Wander under the raised horns of the forklifts at one of the big agricultural fairs and watch a shadowplay of unsuppressed desire: men standing with their faces raised to the polished light of impossible foragers or basking in the afterglow of a succulent JCB. A tractor is the farm's company car. It tells you a lot about both the finances and the mindset of the farmer. And, as with all other vehicles, the strength of a tractor is calculated in horsepower – a clean line of descent from the pulling power of the old form of farm machinery straight towards the new. Two centuries ago, one horsepower was one horse. A century ago, the average tractor could pull around 20 hp. Now, it's maybe 400 to 600 hp. You could, if you chose, now buy something that could comfortably tow a small housing development, so if you're sixteen and sitting on something with the combined pulling power of ten racing stables then no wonder you feel good.

A friend of Ellis has two sons, one of whom has taken a recruitment job in London. According to Ellis, the son only employs people from an agricultural background. The thing about farmers, he says, is that they're adaptable – the human multitools of the professional world. 'You get someone off a farm and they can fix a car, fix a plug, fix a boiler, put their hand in a ewe and pull a lamb out – they're so practically based that he has found in his recruitment world that they're like twice, three times better. So I don't care what our place is or our status. We could do anything.'

Rob's phone goes. Ellis's phone pings. From the next room comes the sound of a small child disagreeing with his sibling.

'You've come here,' says Ellis, getting up. 'And you've seen an affable young man with his miserable old man. And we seem to get on and we have a great time, and we're very lucky that we do get on.' The volume escalates. Ellis raises his voice. 'Do we enjoy it? Yes. It's in the blood.'

10

Title Deeds

A year later.

A year later, there have been changes. As you come up the track now everything looks exactly as it was, except different. Two or three of the old pear trees in the orchard have gone, felled by age and an attack of mistletoe. The polytunnel has vanished, helped along by a winter gale, and the garden itself has been reduced to no more than a couple of raised beds and the Victoria plum. The outbuildings appear just as they were, stacks of feed troughs leaking unobtrusively into the leylandii, the Dutch barn empty and swept. Somebody put the tines of a forklift through the sheep-shed wall, and it has since been patched with a clean piece of tin. Visitors occasionally admired the delicacy with which the many green roofs around the farm have been planted. No planting was ever involved.

David and Alison were thinking about the buildings. The silt and old scrap from Bert's day had gone to the recyclers, the barns had been cleared and a couple of walls had disappeared one night. The derelict blockwork of the old piggery still remained upright, though the tin roof had gone a while ago and the walls now stood naked in a corsetry of bent guttering. David and Alison had put in for permission to turn the buildings into separate accommodation, an idea which had been suggested when Bert was still around but of all his dead-body subjects had been the one most likely to end in a row. As far as Bert was concerned there was no sense in (definitely) spending money now to (possibly) get money in the future. He wasn't keen on the idea of strangers noseying round the farm-yard, parking their cars all over the place, stating the obvious. He didn't see why people might pay extra for the view when the view was neither edible nor refundable, and he wasn't inter-ested in delivering sustainable integration benefits or partnering in positive long-term social-impact outcomes to the kind of people who thought sausages grew in packets. Family, commu-nity, commoners, the parish council and the annual moron visit were, in his view, bad enough, so the idea of a load of townies complaining about funny smells was more than he could take – or at least, more than he could take while also keeping his temper. That half the farm's outbuildings were presently used as a four-bedroom architecturally outstanding dog kennel was beside the point.

David and Alison took a different view. Alison had once run a livestock haulage business and was keen to develop the farm's potential, and David had spent thirty years wanting to try things which his father did not. Both also believed that the only way to shorten the gap between town and country was to draw people in – to show them what happened on farms and who farmers were. Everything now was spread – a bit of B&B, a few sheep, some cows, the SFP, the Stewardship Scheme. Rise Farm wasn't a big enterprise, but then it wasn't in debt either.

A company that made props for films had moved into the workshop. Occasionally I'd return to find someone trimming the talons of a headless pterodactyl or painting in craters on a tiny asteroid. There was a silverback gorilla, a dejected-looking sphinx, and a hoard of gold which looked quite lifelike from the other side of the shed. A half-made space rocket stood propped against a pile of old insulation, and a box labelled

NUCLEAR WASTE was now a biscuit tin. The three people who ran the business had spent a long time making something that was intended to resemble a piece of 200-year-old oak left out in the rain. It had mortice holes and plausible woodworm, but weighed about a tenth of the real thing and smelt of epoxy. The chemicals used to make the composites were violently toxic. Despite wearing permanent ringed circles round their mouths from the indentations of dust masks the staff all had a radioactive tint at odds with the robust good health of the surrounding farm.

In the barn a line of motorhomes and caravans had displaced the old machinery. The owners paid an annual rent to have them housed out of the weather, though the caravans rarely seemed to get used and some had already assumed an air of abandonment. The tractors had been moved to the lower shed, and now stood facing away from the fields in a chronological line. The old Fordson looked like a little greenhouse on wheels; beside it the second-hand New Holland was something designed to plough the wide horizons of Kansas. Children loved to pose by it, since two or three could comfortably be accommodated within the yellow hubs of the back wheels.

For a short while after Bert's death there were no animals except Bryn on the farm, and he was by now almost blind. The last of the old flock had been taken to market when Bert became ill. At the time the decision to sell was a heavy, totemic moment, a declaration – or an admission – that business could not be conducted as usual. Now David and Alison were working the place together, but concentrating on narrowing their risk and keeping the actual farming bit as low-maintenance as possible, treading gingerly. David had bought a few lambs, and then a few more. Six months later he'd got five Hereford beef cows, stolid brickish figures with come-hither lashes and wary brown eyes. Every few days he shifted them from low fields to easy ones, enjoying their enjoyment in the long meadow grass and the nibblings from trees at the edge of the dingle. They were easy calvers who needed little help, and who took well to the steep banks and hidden spaces, vanishing into earth-coloured indistinction on sunless days and moving over the hill with gravitas. David was thinking about getting a bull. Tentatively at first, he was beginning to digress from Bert's purist views on what a farm should be.

11

Breeders

In the big shed forty bull calves are having their balls cut off – a necessary rite of passage, but a noisy one. Jack the stockman is standing in the pen surrounded by a black-and-white scrum of yelling calves and adjusting the barriers of the race to form a funnel down to the crush at the front. Every time he walks a couple of paces half the calves scatter, pinning themselves against the hay bales while the others just stand staring. Outside, the weather glowers. The calves keep up a steady, uneven *wOOoohh*ing, a broken-voiced chorus of dismay, backed by the rattle of rain and the swish of their hooves through the straw.

Down at the front Gavin is tushing the first ones into line. They are wary, disrupted, so Gavin whistles them on – a light musical command, almost birdlike, which helps through familiarity to nudge them into the right place. On the other side of the crush Bill arranges his few essential bits of kit: syringe, spray, scalpel, gloves. Beside us a group of Suffolk ewes stand slit-eyed and impassive, their ears flat as handlebars.

Jack finishes arranging the barriers, swings himself up onto the back of the race and starts sending calves down. At present there are two calves waiting and a little tufty-haired black-and-white bullock at the front. His ears are swivelling with alarm and his eyes are so wide they're almost at right angles. Once Bill is ready Gavin opens the gate at the back, lets the calf through and shuts his neck in the clamp while at the same time twisting his tail round to the side. From the other side Bill reaches over, sticks a needle into the scrotal skin above the calf's testicles, slits the sac with a scalpel, pops each ball out like a bean and then slings it into an old red feed bucket at the side. From the front all that's visible of the calf through the metal gate is his head and his hairy knock knees. As Bill does something the calf can't feel to a bit of his anatomy he's never used, his eyes reach from ease to emergency and then back again. The discarded testes, pale and pink-veined, lie in the bucket like something fished from the bottom of the sea.

Bill sprays the tufty-haired calf's empty scrotum with blue antiseptic and releases the gate at the front. For a stunned two seconds, nothing happens. Then the calf crashes backwards into the guard, kicks twice and shoots forward again, hurtling out towards the light and the big strawed pen at the front. As Gavin lets the next one through, the tufty-haired calf tiptoes away to the dark strawed corners at the side, blue-bummed, a dribble of blood visible beneath his tail. He looks bewildered, incoherent, all his small dignity cut from him.

Bill looks at me looking at the contents of the bucket and laughs. 'Do you want them?'

'Can you eat them?' I say, appalled.

'Suppose so,' says Bill.

'Funny old taste, though, innit?' says Gavin, passing the spray. 'There's a chap near here, loves them. Has three houses, lives in the middle one. Loves them.'

Does it change the bulls' temperament, castration?

'Yes,' says Bill. 'These are dairy calves and dairy bulls are very aggressive.' To Gavin: 'Lim bull, was it?'

Gavin nods.

Are they the worst?

'Yeah,' says Gavin, releasing the handle of the crush to let the next one through. 'Any bull, though. Never trust them. Any of them.'

'Jerseys,' says Bill. 'Jerseys are renowned for being the worst. I got put on the ground two weeks ago.'

For the next few minutes the two men exchange war stories: kickings, crushings, gorings, rearings, things broken or pulled or bruised or hit, blackouts and hospitalisations, cuts or stabs or things that fell on them, whole sections of time or life gone forever. Bill lists the injuries to members of his vet practice while Gavin remembers the bull that went for his father: '... All I could hear was this kerfuffle going on in the cubicle, and there was Father, flat out, bull on top of him, bull pounding his chest, leathering him. I pulled it off him, started shouting, bull turned and ran off. Fair play to Dad, he got up from there and he walked back to the house across the yard just like he'd had a bottle of whisky. He was all over the place, black from top to bottom. And you could see in the black there was darker patches, but he never broke a bone. Hard as bloody nails, Father ...'

Gavin is a solid, wide-faced man with a huge grin, a cheery habit of mind and an unrelenting work ethic. He and his wife Mary run all three farms along with their son-in-law Ben while doing their very best to extract at least forty-eight hours' value out of every twenty-four. And Bill is Bill Main, the vet who had been doing the bTB testing, one of the senior partners at the nearby city practice and a large-animal vet of over thirty years' standing. Gavin was until recently a client of another practice, but swapped when the previous vets changed their pricing structure. Which means that though Bill has only been doing Gavin's vet work for a relatively short period of time he knows Gavin and Gavin's family well – partly because they put a lot of work his way, partly because round here everybody knows everybody, and partly because it's difficult to remain on coolly formal terms while chucking bull testicles past each other.

This is not Bill's first job of the morning at the Whittals' farms and it won't be the last. The appointment combines a scheduled fertility scan, or pregnancy diagnosis (PD), on a group of their dairy cows, these beef castrations, and then a further set of blood checks and PDs on the small herd of suckler heifers run by Gavin's son-in-law. Each appointment is at a different farm. The first was at the dairy on the hill, this is the beef and sheep farm, and the final one of the morning will be at the home farm on the other side of the valley. Including the B&B business, it's something of an empire, built up painstakingly over time first by Gavin's father and now by Gavin and Mary. Not that much trace of it appears online – when I look them up the first thing I find is a 2009 news story about an entirely unrelated Whittal who had been jailed after being found naked up a Tesco chimney.

What's notable about this and many of Bill's other appointments during an average week is how much they're connected with the large-scale administration of fertility. One of the inescapably odd things about farming is just how much time, expense, technology, heartache and devotion is spent by (mostly) men on something so (mostly) female. How much time is spent rummaging around in a ewe's womb, or considering the cycle of laying hens, or poring over the yields from each cow's lactation. For many centuries now most of the space and nearly all of the attention within farming has been taken up with the things that females produce – milk, eggs, lambs, piglets, the next generation, the generations after that. Which means that it's the females which farmers want: the dairy heifers, productive sows, egg-laying hens, nannying goats. They're the ones who ensure both the continuity of the farm and – often – its reason for being. Most experienced livestock farmers will have birthed a thousand babies of one kind or another year after year, and will know considerably more about hormonal fluctuations, uterine disorders and mothering skills than many human medics. Stock farming often looks like obstetrics and gynaecology on a grand scale: the mathematics of multiple lamb births, the geometry of milking parlours, the chemistry of hormones. In fact, much of what used to be called animal husbandry now requires considerably less husbandry than it does midwifery.

With that has come an increasing concentration on the business end (in all senses) of the animal. Look at a farm website these days and the likelihood is that those proud, affectionate pictures of the herd won't show the front end, they'll show you a row of backsides – venous udders cleavaged between black-and-white knees, bagged pink teats splayed out like balloons, double-muscled bulls, their knackers dangling like purses. The size of dairy herds has increased over the past thirty years, as have the yields expected from each cow: 10 litres a day, 20, 30, more. And, since only cows can produce both calves and milk, only cows are useful and thus only cows have any economic longevity.

The flip side of all this concentration on females is a gathering sense that males are becoming optional. At the moment the majority of herds and flocks, including Gavin's, do still keep a bull or a few tups, there being no shortage of pedigree males only too willing to arrange things the old-fashioned way. After all, one tup can impregnate a whole flock of ewes; given weak fencing and a strong will, he'll probably do a lot more. And the bulls will always be there at any agricultural show, patiently chained to a railing while someone pressure-hoses their hooves, there to seduce buyers into admiring the potency of the farm itself.

But beyond a few necessary sperm donors, most stock farms

have no need for a fifty-fifty balance between the sexes. Which means that an increasing number now screen out males before conception, using artificial insemination and sexed semen. It may be more expensive to purchase sperm cells containing the 3.8 per cent extra DNA denoting a female, but if the farm is uninterested in – or doesn't have the land for – rearing a herd of bull steers for beef at the same time as keeping the dairy herd, then it makes sense. After all, who would bother with a full-scale animal when, for half the cost of a major injury lawsuit, he can be replaced by a genetics website selling sperm from Wisconsin?

Farms like Gavin's which still put all their cows to a bull are left with a dilemma. Either they kill the majority of the male calves immediately or they castrate them at a few months old and raise them as beef steers. Due to increasing public concern, some retailers now stipulate on dairy contracts that farmers keep their male calves for at least a year. In other words, Bill's castrations at least ensure Gavin's calves a better, longer and hopefully happier destiny than the alternatives.

A couple of dozen calves further on, Jack has the system work- ing smoothly, the noise level has subsided and we're talking about the best bits of farming. Are there parts that Gavin still enjoys?

'Oh, yeah!' he says, animated. 'Livestock. Livestock, defi- nitely. And getting up in the morning.'

At 4 a.m.?

'But I couldn't get up at seven a.m. – I'd have a bad back!' That huge, full-bodied laugh again. 'Best time of the day. I can't fall out with anybody – nobody to fall out with. I can kick the dog and walk off.'

It's the end of November, a time of year when even the sun

is struggling to rise. If you've got another four hours before it gets light …

'But you can get on. No interruptions.' If he wants a chat, there's always the dog – 'She's the best friend I got.'

Do you ever take holidays?

'Yes.' Momentarily defensive. 'We had three days last year.'

Bill laughs. I laugh. Gavin doesn't. In his view, there's nothing unreasonable about an existence which involves no holidays, mini-breaks, weekends or sick leave. Or which at best involves a short journey to some other part of Britain once every seven years. His experience is not uncommon – many farmers leave the farm only when threatened with full-scale strike action by their partners.

In the three years I knew him Bert Howell only ever took one holiday, a three-day trip to St David's in West Wales which had taken David and Alison five months of painstaking negotiation to arrange. Alison regarded it as a much-needed summer break; Bert saw it as second cousin to abduction. When I asked about it afterwards he said he couldn't remember much about the beach, but he could tell me about the condition of every field between Pontypridd and the Atlantic, and that in his view Carmarthen was behind on its silaging.

Gavin, now: 'A lot of farmers, they don't want to go on holiday. Their holiday is going to market or a show.'

'See, that's the essence of it,' says Bill. 'A farmer is married to the farm, and if you were to marry Gavin, your marriage would not survive unless you married into all these things' – he gestures at the shed, the hill, the calves – 'and you're prepared for Gavin to be out all day and all night …'

Gavin nods.

'… And you're isolated, you don't have any next-door neighbours you can walk round and have a glass of wine with, you live up a drive so there's no passing traffic, there are no holidays because farmers can't do skiing because they're lambing or whatever, and summertime they're harvesting or making hay. It's a totally different life.'

So what are the benefits? It's 24/7, no rest, debt, all that responsibility ...

'Yeah,' says Gavin. 'But if you don't like it, go and be a civil servant.'

But farmers aren't going to sell their farms until their backs are to the wall – they'd feel ...

'... Well, that they'd let their forefathers down, wouldn't they?'

Is that what it is? Disappointing the ancestors?

He laughs, rueful, but whatever he's going to say is interrupted by urgent kicking from within the crush. A five-minute pause while he and Bill move the next ones from the pen to the race.

Did he always want to farm?

Gavin resumes. 'Probably not, no. I wanted to be a policeman or a fireman or an aircraft pilot when I was a boy. But in our day, your future was mapped out for you, really. We didn't ... Well, we did have the option of going to college and that sort of thing, but put it like this: as soon as the bus pulled up at the steps at White House and I was down those steps, I heard Father shouting, "Go and feed the calves, boy!"'

So school wasn't a priority?

Gavin grins. 'Homework was ... you know, that came last if I had to do it, and if I had to do it I didn't usually do it anyway.'

'Have you imposed the same rules on your son?' Bill asks him.

'No,' says Gavin. 'You can't, these days. They've got too much outside. My eldest daughter, she was going to be a veterinary. She went to college and stuck it for three years and she said, "That's it, I don't want no more book work", and came home and got married. It was the theory – she loved being with the animals, but the amount of paperwork these guys have ...'

Bill is feeling through the legs of the next calf, puzzled. 'Gavin?'

'... I know, like Grandma used to say, where there's livestock there's dead stock, but you've got to put up with that – you can't help it. We used to farm and enjoy it, but it's getting harder.'

'Gavin?' says Bill again, frowning.

'Bureaucracy. Just bureaucracy. And the other thing is finance. The worst thing the farmers is up against is finance. The suicides and all the other shit – it's all finances ...'

Bill straightens up.

'If I take animals to the abattoir, supplying them direct, I don't get no job satisfaction out of that. If I take a hundred lambs to market and I can pen them up and they're better than my neighbour's lambs, that's my job satisfaction. And if I can get a good price for them, that even puts the tin hat on it. That's what we done it for.'

'Gavin,' says Bill with finality. 'Are you taking the piss?'

Gavin looks round, startled. 'Say again?'

Bill points down at the calf, leans over and says, 'It's a heifer.'

The heifer looks a little surprised to find the front gate of the crush open and her way clear, but she bounds out and heads for the pen where the little tufty-haired calf is still standing with his companions. Some are in little groups, touching nose-to-nose. Others have their heads down in the thick straw, tails moving queasily.

Gavin puts his hand up, laughing. Outside the shed, it's making a half-hearted effort to snow.

*

A couple of days later, another of his farms. The end of dawn and the day outside is represented only as slats of bruised blue-grey light beyond the cowshed's partitions. It's early winter, and from the different spaces within the shed come early morning sounds: cow's hooves on concrete, a swish of milk through plastic pipes, the plink of a teaspoon, a text alert. The new robot milking system they installed in the dairy a couple of years ago has been acting up. One robot is down and the emergency alarm on the other has been going off every few hours in the middle of the night, which means that Mary and Gavin have been taking it in turns to sleep on the sofa in order to deal with malfunctions. The robot's non-cooperation has also meant an emergency reversion to the old twice-a-day milking system, though a half-and-half regime is itself tricky to timetable.

In the centre of the room is a pen containing around twenty cows arranged herringbone-style with a gate at either end. Each cow is facing towards the wall, its hindquarters overhanging the long narrow alleyway around the edge of the room, meaning that the only thing visible from this particular angle is a row of spattered black-and-white backs and a swivel of ears. The cows are quiet – no shoving, no complaint – but they're also uneasy. When stressed, cows – like humans – will defecate, which means that every few moments another stream of semi-liquid sludge is released onto the rail and the concrete floor.

The cows stand there, shifting their weight from foot to foot. Bill, now dressed in a green plastic apron, pulls on a pair of long-sleeved plastic gloves in a surprising shade of tutu pink and starts working his way down the line of backs. On his head he is wearing something that looks like a cross between a high-tech virtual reality headset and a pair of horn-rimmed reading glasses. The headset covers the top portion of his vision, with little flicky shutters which can be pushed up or down depending

Breeders

on whether he wants to see one kind of world (the ultrasonic one), or both. Holding a probe, he lifts each tail and pushes his arm up to the elbow along the cow's rectum. He's talking over his shoulder while rummaging around for a while inside the cow as if groping for pipework under a car bonnet. Once in a while, he glances over his shoulder at a sludge-spattered monitor screen.

'She's bulling,' he says.

Mary notes something on her clipboard.

Bill pulls out the probe, washes, inserts the probe up the next one.

This one is in calf. On her clipboard, Mary makes a small + sign beside the cow's tag number. 'How long?'

Bill peers upwards into the headset. 'Couple of weeks?'

The next. 'Dirty.' An infected uterus, the result perhaps of a previous pregnancy which never fully cleaned itself out. 'Was she examined?'

Mary looks at the list. A consultation, a plan. They move on.

Two more in calf. Then an empty – no pregnancy, and no sign of oestrus. Any cow not already pregnant or ready to be put to the bull is described as empty or barren, a minus by her name. Whereas the language for human fertility has evolved into something more sparing, farming, as always, retains its unpeeled honesty: bulling, calving, barren, dirty, empty, maiden. A barren cow – one which has dried off after a previous lactation but which cannot become pregnant, cannot calf and therefore cannot produce milk – is no use to a dairy.

Bill squints into the headset. Mary hovers between the cows and the monitor, though all I can see is incoherence – a cryptic fuzz of light and dark which looms or dwindles as Bill moves the probe.

'See the head?' he says. A blare of light.

Field Work

'Sort of,' I say, uncertain.

A curve, a rambling horizon line, a sparkle like a distant star enclosed in its own galaxy.

To Mary and Bill, everything is perfectly legible – a leg, a twin, an absence. Good, better, bad. Zero, plus, minus. Bill moves steadily down the line. This is one of his regular visits – a quick scheduled PD test on a few dozen of the farm's cows. This place has a contract with Tesco, meaning that the business of fertility is not seasonal but year-round. What all supermarkets want most of all is absolute consistency of supply. At different times of year they might require more milk or less, but the quality should be identical every time. In return they'll guarantee a cost-of-production price (say, 26 pence per litre) plus an extra fee for the farmers' labour. And if things do go very wrong – illness among the herd, labour shortages – the supermarket might have a conversation about how to sort the problem out, but it will also reserve the right to cancel the contract at any time. The benefit to any farmer who can deliver is a steady price and a reliably insatiable customer; the drawback is relentless dependency.

Overlying the sound of the cows in here is the lull of the machines next door. In the cubicle between the old milking parlour and the shed are the two robotic milkers. They are large, red, Swiss, very sophisticated, and very expensive. The machine acts as a partition between this room and the big shed and, as I watch the open space at the bottom of the partition, the lower half of a cow walks across it and stops. The red sniper dot of a laser tracer flickers against the four quarters of her udder, locating the position of each teat. The robot washes her down, positions each of the four milkers directly below the relevant teat and lifts the milkers into place. The cow seems content, unfazed either by the clicks and whirrings or by the mechanical stall. She, like all the others, is wearing an electronic tag around her neck which gets scanned as she walks in. Once recognised, her biometric information is fed into the system and the exact position of each milker adjusted accordingly. The cow stands there, patient, while her milk empties out through four clear tubes into the tank next door. Once she's done the robot sprays her down again, removes itself and releases the gate. She moves out to join her companions before returning to her stall. Behind her the next cow walks in.

Inside the big shed most of the cows are lying ruminating within their individual partitions. All that's visible from the edge is the occasional flick of an ear or the soft curve of a belly rising. There's 400 in here, but almost no noise. Just the automated ticks of the robots and an occasional scuffle as one of the cows finds the scratching brush and gives herself a good itch.

Under the old twice-a-day system cows would spend most of their time grazing out in the fields and be brought in morning and afternoon to be milked. Under this system the cows are permanently indoors but can choose to be milked at any time. Given a decision in the matter, many elect to be milked three or four times a day, queueing briefly whenever they feel like it rather than according to the necessities of a shift pattern. And, true to the laws of unintended consequences, the advent of robots within an increasing number of dairy businesses has apparently altered other things as well. In some places it has changed the dynamics between cows, smoothing out the hierarchies and reducing the gap between dominant cows and milder ones. Under the old system the more extrovert characters would barge to the front to get milked or fed first while the meeker ones got stuck at the back. Under the new one, that levelling has also meant less of a difference in the cows' physical condition: the small ones are bigger, and the big ones are smaller.

Robot-induced social equality or not, each of these cows is still expected to pull her weight in milk. Any dip below around 30 litres a day would be noted; any continuing dip might necessitate removal for slaughter. All dairy herds work on lactation periods, with the aim being to get at least one calf per cow every fourteen months or so. Thus a two-year-old heifer has her first calf, the calf is taken away almost immediately after birth, milking starts, and she is then put to the bull (served) again as soon as she is ready. After a length of time (usually around seven months), the cow is 'dried off' for a couple of months, allowing her to rest. The cycle repeats for several more lactations until the cow is finally retired at around six or seven years old. In all, a British dairy cow would probably average around 7,500 litres in her lifetime. In America that would be over 10,000 litres, and in Israel between 12,000 and 14,000 litres. The current dairy cows now convert far more of their diet into milk, while beef cows – who generally live outside on grass and keep their calves by them for five or six months – convert their food into meat.

Fifty miles away in Shropshire Nick Gibbon, who works at the same practice as Bill Main, is at a large dairy farm with 400 cows calving all year round. The farm is rented by Sam Sawtrey off the Duchy Estate and is run by him in partnership with his father, this time supplying Waitrose.

Nick is cheery, practical, vigorous. Mid-thirties, delighted to work with like-minded souls, completely engaged with both the physical work and the software. Bits of modern vet work are boring, he concedes, but so is any job. 'The best jobs are the night ones,' he says, shooing a couple of cows into the stall. 'Three a.m., going out to a calving or an emergency – the hero calls, the ones where you really make a difference to the outcome.'

After PD'ing twenty-odd heifers, Nick sits down with Sam

and herdsman Novak to pick through a new piece of software which will offer the farm a complete analysis of each animal in statistical form – age, health, productivity, average daily milk yield, number of lactations.

This whole herd is also under a TB restriction. In public terms that restriction doesn't have much of an impact – all milk products from here would be pasteurised anyway, removing any trace of the disease long before it reached a human – but in private, it's as difficult here as it is on any other farm. Every sixty days when the test comes around they lose several good cows and the disease keeps herds effectively quarantined in isolation, stagnating any chance of breed development. Sam can only put his cows to his own bulls, or to those from other closed herds. At the moment he's preoccupied with pushing up his milk's fat content; if he was able put them to bulls from other herds he might be able to tweak the content faster. Waitrose isn't asking for it, but the middlemen Müller and Arla are.

Since all of Sam's herd's DNA has been tested, every cow's individual data can be broken down according to individual gene characteristics or its place in the overall herd genomics. Because a closed herd may be served by the same bull or bulls for many years, there's a strong risk of in-breeding: same father, grandfather, great-great-great-grandfather, though even with open herds many of the cows will be either directly or closely related to each other. That too can now be tested, screened for, the rogue markers flagged. Each cow here produces an average of 38 litres a day, and they can now examine that milk according to its protein, fat, mineral or vitamin content, its chemical presentiments of disease or infection, its hormonal shiftings. They could even tell you – in physical terms at least – how happy or unhappy that cow appears to be.

In the past a good farmer might have been able to work all of those things out by observation based on 'feel' and experience, 'feel' being a mixture of bovine psychology, translation of body language and the more direct physical clues: skin condition, weight, alterations in yield. All of that still applies – the herdsman Novak knows the majority of his cows by name, habits and parentage, but he, Nick and Sam will also spend as much time staring at a screen as they do at a cow. Keeping each cow in peak health and at peak production levels is not easy; these are the thoroughbreds of the bovine world. An average of 38 litres per day per cow is a knife-edge level of production, and though some will be above that and some below, a state of constant watchfulness needs to be maintained by both human and software.

'She's got good fat,' says Nick at one point, looking at the figures for one third-lactation cow. 'Good fertility, a good lifespan, she's moderate for milk. She's not going to set the world alight, but she's an OK cow.'

Sam points at the screen. 'That one,' he says. 'Two six four. Not great – the only thing dragging her up is her milk.'

Listening to them, I think they talk about the cows the way large organisations talk about their employees – background, performance, output, characteristics. Admittedly, most organisations do not eat their worst performers, but the mindset is similar. Cows/staff are a resource. A precious one, filled with wonder and singularity, but still. A resource.

When I put this to Nick Gibbon, he protests, vehement. 'This is true; they are a resource, but they're also not objectified to this extent. Sam and quite a few other dairy farmers build a bond with their animals, they respect them, and I know that he cannot be on the yard to load his animals when they go to the abattoir. Many dairy farmers can't bring themselves to do it. It's a strange bond that's formed, similar to the shepherd and his favourite bitch. She may live in a shed, chained up at night with straw for a bed if she's lucky, but if anything happens to her the shepherd is much more distraught than your average non-working-pet owner. There is something about what they have shared and their working environment which is often alone, cold, wet, hard, early, late. It creates a bond beyond man and beast that very few can claim to have experienced. The cow is not really working for them: they're working for her. They're there to see all of her daughters born, to lift her from the yard if she falls, to treat her if she is unwell. If they don't do a good job of these things, then she won't produce the milk which allows them to continue. Sam is a clever man: a university education, a good head for numbers, a clear understanding of most aspects of my job as well as his own, yet he chooses to be in the most volatile, profitless and persecuted sector of food production because of this unique symbiosis that, even though I work in it day after day, I struggle to describe with words.'

Certainly all the cattle farmers I spoke to, whether beef or dairy, were single-mindedly devoted to their herds, whether that was 300 high-yield Holstein-Friesians in a state-of-the-art roboticised facility or a million-guinea clutch of pedigree Limousins. All of them were as proud and concerned as parents, and in every single case the herd came first. If really pushed, most would have had genuine difficulty choosing between their partners and their cows, and in several cases it wouldn't have worked out well for the partner.

Which leads on to another point. While farmers – male or female – may well spend an impressive amount of time on the logistics of group sex, their own love lives often leave a lot to be desired. In the past, farmers would grow up on a farm, the oldest male would inherit, he would choose a wife preferably from a farming background herself, they would go on to have lots of little farmers. Or that was the theory. But, natural selection being what it is, some families only had daughters, or had no children at all, or the son didn't want to farm. Or, just as possible, the son couldn't find a wife.

12

Futures

In addition to the many speciality online dating sites now available (Christian, rich, old, tall, small, gluten-free, long-term secure), there are also those which have evolved to cater to farming's determinedly niche breeding criteria. And, just as not everyone in life is after a sugar daddy or a shy bearded Russian with an interest in shoes, not every lover is necessarily seduced by the sight of a plumb-straight plough line or a one-ton Charolais. Not everyone wishes to have their home as a business or spend the majority of their life dressed in the kind of clothes designed to be easily hosed. Most of all, not everyone is prepared to live in happy triangular coexistence with that other presence: the farm.

The dating site Muddy Matches has a field gate as a logo and a rural aspect to its searches. From the beginning its aim has been to appeal to the broadest reach of country folk it possibly can, from the entirely agricultural to confirmed urbanites who like large SUVs but remain unsure of intelligent life beyond the M25. Some of its members are farmers, but there are also many who are living in or commuting to cities. The aim being, as its co-founder Lucy Reeves puts it, to appeal to 'nice, normal people'. At present the site has around 200,000 members, though not all are active at one time – people will sign up, appear, disappear, reappear, all according to their own private schedules of needs and desires.

The website was started by two sisters, Lucy and Emma Reeves, who grew up in Northamptonshire and, after careers abroad (Lucy working as a Spanish translator, Emma as a marine biologist), moved back to the UK. Emma returned home to the farm, and Lucy lived for a time in London.

At the time, says Lucy, both were on their own, 'and Emma was moaning about being single and living in the middle of nowhere. And I was saying, "Oh, there must be a dating site", and she was saying, "But everyone's so *townie*." And I was saying, "There must be something for country people."'

There wasn't. It was 2006, and online dating was just beginning to move from something used only by nerds meeting other nerds into something willingly mainstream. A few years before they started it, online dating was still considered 'the domain of freaks and weirdos'; a few years later, the market was saturated. Neither sister had any business background or any experience of setting up websites. They found a designer, sketched out their ideas, built the site, tweaked it, and were on their way. It took them a while to learn what worked and what didn't (nothing involving unrealistically high broadband speeds, apps tricky). The idea was the source of some bewilderment among their friends – 'they thought it wouldn't work and that it was a crap name' – but once they had hit on the right formula, they succeeded enormously.

The company's office is in a converted brick byre beside a livery stable near the farm where Lucy and Emma grew up. The village itself is Cotswold-pretty, content and preserved, but the landscape surrounding it feels meek and de-wilded. Here in the warehoused centre of Britain, just off the motorway but convenient for transport links, there are no awkward curves or hills, no mountains; nothing to break the symmetry of a fence line or the height of a sky. Farms are big arable agri-businesses, acred by the thousand, defined by straight-edged fields ploughed and ploughed again over, year after year, a harrowing as old as Domesday. It feels like a place without unknowns, a place defined just as much by lines and coordinates as by the old dictatorship of seasons. The village overlooks a broad landscape of water towers, mobile masts, creeping suburbs and 20-acre logistics hubs. This is middle Britain, the flat fully employed centre, strung with pylons and conquered with warehouses. At its heart is a lacework of necrotic old motorways offering a perpetual route to somewhere not here. The further you creep east the less the green bits look like country and the more they look like landscaping, negative spaces which no one's quite got around to building on yet.

The business's HQ acts as a perfect representation of the sisters' priorities. The office seems tentative and half-used; a void with one person in it, a room containing nothing but dead tech and empty dog baskets. When I arrive Lucy is in a meeting and the only other member of staff is going through profiles in an area partitioned with felt-lined boards on which are pinned photos of the site's key achievements – wedding, baby, wedding, baby, wedding, wedding, spaniel, spaniel, farm machinery – sent in by satisfied customers.

The website, by contrast, is where the attention is. If it was a house it would be rambling, traditional, well-lived – nothing flashy or novel, scuffed in places but cared-for. Things which were put down in one space have been given the occasional dusting but left untouched for years, while other parts bear the marks of many passings.

Lucy is forty, blonde, energetic, and dressed in don't-care country kit – navy top, long silver necklace, jeans, leather boots. She spends quite a bit of our meeting with her arms folded, not quite at ease, pulling her long hair back from her face, gathering it, spinning it round a finger. Though not unfriendly, she is obviously more preoccupied with protecting the brand than saying much. Which makes sense – they've got no need to sell Muddy Matches. It is a huge success, and it stands alone. As she points out, there are other sites now specialising in aspects of rural dating, but they maintain their near-monopoly simply by having the largest pool of singles from which to pick.

Specific pages on the site do deal with both farmers and equestrians – 'We've got a lot of horsey members.' In both cases the advice – often written by members – can be affectionate but demoralising: 'Remember that you come second … Worst time to date a farmer is when the milk price drops … don't even think of planning anything during the harvest … often smell of poo'.

When the Reeves started, they had one idea of what rural life meant (shooting, tweed), but 'actually, it's so much broader'. By concentrating on the concept of muddiness (do you identify as 100 per cent agricultural, or are you geographically non-binary?) they broadened it beyond just 'people like us'. 'Now we've got a huge amount of people who are just really outdoorsy, or they live in a city and aspire to live in the countryside. They dream of getting a smallholding one day and want to find someone to do it with.'

Unsurprisingly, they do get some people on the site who have seen the cookery programmes, tasted the artisanal pork and 'think they want the farming life because they have this vision of it being all black labs and Agas and driving Range Rovers – very *Emmerdale*. But the reality is that there's no such thing as a farmer's wife staying home and baking cakes: usually, they'll have a part-time job at Tesco.'

I thought of the hands of the women at the livestock market. Still beautiful, and certainly eloquent, but every line and ache descriptive of hard work. Another image. Listening to the chug of the quad on days when Bert and Alison were doing the morning round together. Once or twice a week they rode back up the track through the rain, Alison perched on the back with her arm around Bert's waist. There was something about the way they leaned together and the care with which he eased up the throttle that seemed to say a lot about partnership.

Why did the sisters feel that there was a need for this? Only around 9 per cent of Britain's total land area is urban and yet country folk, Lucy says, are 'more [niche] than any other niche I know of, although I suppose religion is probably the closest'. Farming is a niche within a niche. In emotional terms there's nothing different about someone who works on the land – they fret and laugh like the rest of us do. But practically, they often have a lengthy list of must-haves and non-negotiables: must be prepared to move to the farm, must be good with animals, must have a head for business. In practice, a date with a farmer is often less a romantic encounter than a searching interview for a long-term administrative position in a far-off part of the country.

Asked what else is unique, Lucy points to farming's reputation for directness. At one stage the site launched a section called Newest Members, and when she was running an event shortly afterwards, 'a farmer came up to me and said, "I like the Fresh Meat counter."'

And for farmers more than most, a website makes a life beyond seem suddenly possible. In the early days, Lucy and Emma used to organise meet-up events in different parts of the country until one dairy farmer pointed out to her that the milking schedule made leaving the farm almost impossible. 'It can be just too complicated, organising the cover.' The sisters eventually gave up on the events because it was so difficult to please people. They'd be told that it was in the wrong place or the wrong part of the country, or no one had met anyone they fancied. Or they didn't get on with the person they were sitting next to, or there's an age issue –'men in their fifties only want to meet women of child-bearing age, but you think, "No, I'm not going to put you next to some bored twenty- or thirty-year-old woman.'"

Happily, Lucy's own life mirrored that of the site. When the business started to take off she decided to leave London and come back to Northamptonshire. 'There's always that idea in my background that you went away to work and you meet someone and then you move back and settle down if you want to have a family. And so I ended up moving back before meeting anyone, five years into doing Muddy Matches, living in the countryside, thinking, "Crikey, how do I meet someone?"'

So what happened?

'I was lucky – I met my husband online.'

What, on Muddy Matches?

No, she says – neither she nor Emma ever joined their own site because 'it just seemed a bit unethical'. Instead, she tried a rival site, and found someone 'on the fresh meat counter'. He is now her husband. 'I was the first person he had met up with – so either he's not very picky, or it was just really good luck.'

She and Emma now run the farm in partnership with their brother, who takes care of the day-to-day management while they deal with the business.

On the way out we both stand in front of the board looking at the pictures: women in white smiling from the front seat of tractors, newborns radiant on haybales. 'Our first Muddy Matches baby is ten now,' Lucy says wonderingly.

Looking at the images it does seem an astonishing thing, to have played a small part in the redirection of so many lives, to have been the agent of so many relationships, to have formed so many connections and solved so many compatibility issues, to have caused love or to have made love's wider distribution possible. All dating sites have their critics – by the law of averages, there must be as many creeps and players in the country as in the city – but it seems a profound achievement to see as part of your life's work a board filled with optimism and new human beings.

For many within agriculture Young Farmers still performs the same function as Muddy Matches, though this time for free and in person. Many generations of farmers have met through the YF's events – clubs, parties, lock-ins, tents at the big agricultural shows. And there is still (will always be) space for relationships formed in the stands at county shearing competitions. Either way, the advantages of Young Farmers are first, that it's local, meaning there's already a good chance that one farm would be known to another, and secondly, that everyone knows that while it's lovely to talk about the rugby and/or the upsides in surveying with drones, its main purpose is to facilitate the perpetuation of an agricultural dynastic line through the liberal application of beer.

In many areas, though, YF doesn't play the same role it did in the past. Its reputation as somewhere that allowed under-age drinking lured in townies and horsey people, which meant that in many areas the rules got changed and parental consent forms were required. And, where once YF had a monopoly, it no longer does – partly through online dating apps, partly through wider travel generally, and partly because it now has competition.

The other tested route to marriage is through agricultural college. For many families it is now taken as a rite of passage either to go to one of the main colleges within the UK, or to take contract work elsewhere to get experience, see something of the world outside The Farm and earn some decent money.

Harper Adams University in Shropshire is one of the UK's

two best-known agricultural universities, offering courses from zoology to food technology. Cirencester – older, posher – is the other. Like Cirencester, Harper's basic course, the thing for which the place is known, is agriculture. Sometimes that's just agriculture, but often it comes with add-ons: land science, business management, marketing. It aims to teach students how to work land or to lure a living from it, though if there is a shorthand way to understand the difference between the two colleges it's probably that Cirencester teaches people how to inherit a farm while Harper teaches them how to run it.

In looks and style Harper is no different to other universities – institutional Victorian red-brick warted with later add-ons, noticeboards patched with excitable flyers, municipal planting. The only difference is in the details. Not all universities have fibreglass Friesians on their pavements or 635 hectares of unbuilt land on which to experiment, or a student bar called the Welly Inn. And relatively few undergraduates at Russell Group universities start conversations with, 'You know that armoured personnel carrier I was driving the other day? Yeah? Well, I broke it.' If this was the army, then Harper Adams and Cirencester would be agriculture's Sandhurst, the place where the twenty-first century's executive officers are drilled and grilled and fitted up for leading. This is not the place where the grunts get to go – the potato graders and fruit pickers, the ones who have no say in the farm's future. This place and Cirencester are training the individuals who will most mark the British countryside.

I contacted the university, explained, and asked if there were any students who would be happy to talk. Eight students volunteered, equally split between male and female, and ranging in age from twenty to twenty-seven. The majority were from farming backgrounds, but only one of the eight would inherit a farm. As part of their degrees all students do a year's placement, though each had also accepted the need to train for other work either as a preamble to or substitute for a return to the land. Though most of them were impatient to try out new ideas, they saw time working elsewhere as a healthy part of the process, a chance to gain an alternative view of the world. Many also felt themselves exceptional among their peers. Several of the students had grown up on farms, but the people around them – schoolfriends or siblings, the same people who fifty years ago might never have considered any other life – were often mystified by the concept of farming as a career. To them it seemed a bit weird, a bit retrogressive, like choosing to be a housewife, or choosing to be broke.

Matthew Rollaston is twenty-two and specialising in bovine genetics. He's not from a farming background himself, so back at home he's had a lot of explaining to do: 'They don't see it. It's, "Why would you want to be a farmer?" A little bit jokey, a little bit puzzled, but just, "Why?"'

I think of Wales. When Bert had been at the village school in the 1950s, half his year had gone into farming. When David was at the same school in the 1990s, only four in his year did. Some parents of Harper students had actively tried to deter their children from following them. If those parents were themselves farmers then the resistance was often one born of broken experience – effectively, don't follow us down. And from friends, it was connected to status. Why would you want to do a cold, wet, filthy job working with your granddad at stupid times of day for no money when your peers were selling houses and clocking off at 5 p.m.? OK, so you got to work from home, but plenty saw that as an active disadvantage.

Back in Bert's day farming had stood solid at the centre of national life. Post-war Britain, just released from the German wolfpacks and the threat of starvation, was only too aware of the meaning of food security. But as the workforce dwindled, farming, the most visible profession of all, retreated back over the hedge. As the cities spun faster and faster, pulling more and more of that rural workforce away from the country, the profession folded into itself, mistrustful and resigned.

Many of the Harper Adams students had already spent years trying to persuade either their families or their peers that agriculture could mean something more than a lifetime of bad weather – that a career in environmental monitoring or seed genetics was just as possible as making stripes on fields. All are also at pains to point out that agriculture and farming are not synonyms. Farming (the business of growing crops and raising livestock) is only one branch of agriculture (the science and art of cultivating plants and animals). Which in turn means that a seed geneticist, a hydrographer or an arborist can still be working within agriculture even if they never go near a tractor.

Some of the outside resistance to farming is connected to its appalling mental health record. Another student, Rowan Boardley, is doing Agriculture and Land Sciences. She read Physics at Imperial in London and then thought about becoming a vet, but at the last minute she came here instead. As part of her most recent placement for a feed company she was going onto farms with volunteers from the Royal Agricultural Benevolent Institution or the Farming Community Network. 'Sitting here now, you think everything's fine,' she says. 'But then you get on a farm and you're sitting with someone asking them to sign a cheque for nine grand, twenty grand, because they're behind on the payments, and you're thinking, "I can't be asking them to do this", because you know they're not making enough money. And some people, they dig a hole so deep. But they just cover it with pride.'

At twenty-seven Jack Poulden is the oldest. He came to this from a previous career, is the most political of the students, and radiates an almost combustible fervour. 'Farming has got all the risk factors,' he says. 'Low wages, high risk, high mortality, working on your own, working under pressure most of the time, isolation ... I think people probably just need to feel hope, that you're doing something worthwhile. And at the moment, with the situation the industry is in, there's a lot of negativity. You need to feel like you're winning a bit.'

Matthew agrees. 'The way things are now, I wouldn't look at agriculture and want to be a farmer. It's not striking me as a good future. I don't want to spend sixteen hours a day working for peanuts and taking forty years getting to where I want to be.'

Several of the Harper students point out that farmers often get together young and may not have a chance to broaden their experience of society. In most workplaces, overt misogyny would have been wormed out long ago. In farming, it's still there, living like dry rot under the beams. Rowan: 'I go out to farms as part of my job, and I can be talking to a farmer who's thirty or sixty-five and the difference in – not in respect, but in willingness to listen to my ideas – is huge. Because the older generation, they see, "First of all, you're young, and secondly, you're a woman. So you cook my dinner and you wash my clothes." It's ridiculous.'

'We were just talking about farmers' sons and daughters marrying,' says Jack Poulden. 'The level of inbreeding sometimes is so ...' – he tails off to general laughter – 'and if you carry on that metaphor, what do you get? You generally get a weaker, failing line. You get line-breeding weakness.'

You also get very little diversity. It's telling that if you search for 'diversity in farming' online, what comes up is not material on those from a minority background, but diversification. If you search further, all that comes up is information on how to start a llama business.

Field Work

Down the road at Harper's competitor Cirencester, Navaratnam Partheeban is a senior lecturer in livestock production, but also very much an outlier in his own land, one of a tiny number of non-white UK vets, an even tinier number of non-white farm vets, and probably one of only one Scottish large-animal vets who have the academic background to lecture on the subject. Somewhere in the long hard haul up to his current position (a tiny attic room overlooking a view of buttery Cotswold Victoriana) he has also taken in practices in Wales and Somerset and a detour into the pharmaceutical industry.

He's thirty-six, round-faced, friendly and very, very determined. As he points out, it hasn't just been sustained ignorance from the farming and veterinary communities he's had to deal with, it's opposition from within his own family. His parents were first-generation immigrants from Sri Lanka and Malaysia who wanted a doctor for a son, not a vet. A standard medical degree would almost certainly have given him an easier ride: 40 per cent of UK doctors are from BAME backgrounds, though only 3 per cent of vets are, and the majority of those will be in small-animal practice.

When he met me in Cirencester's reception area, we walked over to the café past groups of students sitting out in the sun between lectures. Though there were just as many female students as male, every single one was white. And, as Navaratnam points out, 'The lack of diversity is itself a deterrent to diversity.' The lack of role models becomes a self-perpetuating problem, since if other black or Asian students take a look at an apparently monocultural profession, what they see is not just the work they'll do but the mountain of assumptions they'll have to climb every working day. When he describes his own long journey to Cirencester, through practices where he felt properly supported (Wales), and places where he didn't (Somerset), it sounds at times both lonely and exhausting.

Having faced direct racism on farms, and occasionally from his fellow vets, he looked for support from professional bodies, and was initially told either that it was someone else's problem or that no one there could advise on it since they hadn't faced it themselves. Hence the two-year 'holiday' in pharmaceuticals, where for once he wasn't alone. 'We had vets coming in from France, Germany, Spain, Brazil. It was really diverse and nice, and I never felt like I was on my own. When Europeans saw me, it was the first time I was called British.' After he tweeted about a racist letter he had received, 'a load of Scottish people emailed me and said, "Come back home! Come back to your own country!" It's the nicest thing someone could have said to me.'

Instead, he returned to the fray, lecturing at Cirencester and working to change the industry.

Does he feel that the racism he encountered came from real hatred, or from ignorance and lack of exposure?

'The genuinely racist, really extreme people are a tiny minority,' he says. 'The group of ignorant people is slightly bigger, but the majority of people are willing to put their hands up and say, "I don't understand, but can you teach us or explain to us?" The current generation, more exposed through social media to experiences other than their own, are beginning to move away from the attitudes of their parents, but there's still that mountain every day.' The solution, Navaratnam thinks, is to shift the structure of both farming and independent vet practice away from single-cell units and towards cooperatives: 'Working together, not being isolated and just working on your own, is the way forward.'

And so, inevitably, to Brexit. If there are aspects of farming which need shaking up, then it may well be Britain's withdrawal from the EU which provides the disruption. If millennials generally tend to be more Remain than Leave, then the students at Harper Adams reverse that. All eight students I spoke to regarded Brexit as an opportunity, their logic being that if it also meant the phasing out of most agricultural subsidies, then the bottom 20–30 per cent of farms would go out of business. These interviews were done before Covid-19 had changed the economic landscape and the withdrawal of government funding slid from a probability to an inevitability, but even then, within both farming and government, there seemed to be a consensus: removal of BPS and other schemes would strip out anything from a fifth to a third of Britain's holdings. The headline in that week's *Farmer's Guardian* over a piece discussing the DEFRA view of the future was 'Let Them Fail'. Once those holdings went, then, as the Harper Adams students saw it, new, young tenants would either be able to take over the tenancy, or – even, wildly – to take over the mortgage and move in. It was a rationale which did not account for the strong possibility that larger landowners in the area would simply claw up the smaller ones, as had happened in many areas with the sale of council farms. But what it did measure was the ravening hunger of a younger generation to break the grip of the past.

So if all payments were withdrawn, would that benefit younger farmers?

Jack Poulden: 'God, yeah. Just look at the industry – it's dying.'

Rowan Boardley: 'It will be the marginal ones, it will be the laggards in every sector – dairy farms, sheep farms. The lowest 25 per cent will lose out, and that will open out opportunities for everyone in terms of tenancies and land.'

Matthew Rollaston: 'And it's not that we want Armageddon and for it all to turn to dust, but if people have resisted change and they haven't worked with it and they can't see their own demise, then that's their own demise, I'm afraid.'

None of the students thought of this as a personal battle.

They understood the older generation's need to hold on and the resistance to change, but they also maintained a refreshing ruthlessness towards their future profession. What was viable about an industry where the entry fee (the cost of land) was well over a million, but the income was often less than £10,000 a year? And what was good about a system where cheap food was only possible because the poorest farmers were effectively propped up by benefits?

The undertone humming beneath all of this is impatience – impatience at a decrepit system, impatience to get on, impatience to change. What I've heard are the frustrations, but that's just a light topping over the idealism and energy coming up from below. If anything, the obstacles only make them more certain that there is a better way of doing things. Which, of course, has been the birthright of every new generation since civilisation began. In the end, it all connects to a sense of significance – to feel that each day's work has produced a visible difference, to have planted out the future or changed in some way a corner of this land. Despite the obstacles there is something so barefacedly simple about growing food for people to eat that it overrides everything in its path.

That clarity is most clearly visible in their hopes. At the end of the conversation I asked all the students what their dream was – not their ambition, but their money-no-object, reality-no-problem fabulous future.

Emily Jones: 'My own small farm.'

Rowan: 'If I could have a couple of acres, I'd have some sheep.'

Luke Ormond: 'Not have to work that often and have a house in the Lake District with a few cows.'

Thomas Whittaker: 'Go home and have it all.'

What they wanted was an old, old dream. All were practical about their career paths, whether that was deep-sea mining or supply-chain management, but all of them dreamed of having a family-sized smallholding – a patch of land, maybe a brook. Sometimes there were pigs or sheep in there or a vineyard, maybe it was a business, or perhaps just a way to sustain a few precious individuals. But always there was stock. It was a dream as old as life, and as I left I wondered if I'd gathered together a group of Wall Street bankers or tech company execs if I wouldn't have got exactly the same answer.

Epilogue

A new year. Floods. Five months of almost continuous rain. River levels consistently overtopping the high-water gauges. Familiar places have become exotic: a pond where a brook used to be, a loch where a river once was, a sea stationary where a river had moved, a brook bedded over a B-road. People treat a school run or a journey to work with the same death-or-glory spirit as an ascent of K2, knowing that if they go out they may be some time. Down in the valley the churches are flooded and the pubs surrounded. Cars and shipping containers float past at a steady 5 knots, unperturbed by obstacles. Houses, shops, garages – all have become foreign lands, divided by impassable waters, one side of the valley now as separate from the other as England is from France. Everybody worries about their engine flooding; everyone secretly wonders how to get hold of a tractor. Along the main roads, low spots silt with clusters of freshly drowned cars while swans sail through the school car parks.

Farmland too has altered in interesting ways. What had once been prime lowland arable has in several places transformed itself into large inland lakes sliced by random hedge lines. From above everything takes on a levelled, abstract quality: black trees against silvered liquid, fences submerged, nothing but branches still visible. Only the occasional tell-tale sign – parallel lines, a half-formed bridge – shows where the rivers once belonged. In the higher fields the gullies of each plough line shine against the sky. When occasionally the rain does stop the water doesn't move. It just stands there, reflecting.

Field Work

Up on its 900-ft cloud, Rise watches over it all. The sheep are mostly still out, standing trench-footed, their lower halves blending so indivisibly with the colour of the mud that from a distance they look like large turnips. In some of the empty pastures water springs from the ground from places it never has before, rising from below as if the grass is only a lid. Through the swirl of winter fog, the sound of rain running is always audible. Half a mile further along the lane the ground has given way, sliding resignedly down the hill, taking the road and the access to three houses with it. At night the pour of water appears as a soft white blur of sound, the only thing audible against the laden sky.

In the higher fields the Hereford cows and their new calves (won ten, lost one) stand beneath the trees. Both the mothers and the calves look unwrapped, exposed to too many elements all at once. Two of the cows have had Caesareans and now sport large shaved rectangles on their flanks. The calves – still rickety and surprised – headbutt their mothers' udders in search of milk. A mile away on the opposite hill a black-and-white line of Friesians, let out for the first time this spring, move in line across the slope with the care of a police search team.

After a gap of several years, the lights in the big shed have been on again this March. David has resumed both lambing and calving, only this time with the addition of technology. Night watches have been made easier by the installation of a GoPro camera, meaning David can check on any developments from the farmhouse kitchen. The vet has been out once, the knacker a couple of times, and the holiday rental photographers have made complimentary noises about the view. The building work on the old yard has nearly finished, and the place has been getting good reviews online – 'very friendly … couldn't do enough for us … great hot tub … love the dog and the cat'. David is hedging his bets – ninety sheep, thirty cows, the rented grazing, the cottage, Airbnb, Single Farm Payment, writing (What about? 'Depression and cheese, mostly') and, as he puts it, becoming 'Wales's go-to composer of songs about farm animals'. He's doing a counselling degree, planning to use the farm both as a place of work and a source of healing in itself. He's getting married soon; his fiancée Anna is expecting twins.

The rain stops and the sun comes out. As the floodwater recedes, Covid-19 advances. For a while, all discussion of quarantines, infection rates, curfews and lockdowns appears as the same background fuzz as other news, a backdrop to the traditional start-of-year business: ploughing, sowing, government inquiries. As the sound of rainwater slips from a rush to a drip to a silence the noise from outside swells, advancing fast from international to national to local, taking on shape and specificity, arming itself with threats and laws. The government finds itself defending against an invisible enemy, a danger contained within human behaviour and spread by the things which make us humane: touch, kindness, proximity, trust. Even before full lockdown on 23 March, agricultural workers and vets are put on a list of essential workers. Almost everything else – schools, offices, suppliers – closes.

For a long time there are no sounds in the country except tractors and birdsong. The hospitality industry ceases overnight. There are no pubs or hotels to sell local produce, no flights to bring us flowers, no sit-down chips or teatime treats. In the shops, people stockpile. Everyone has to eat in, which means supermarkets are also providing ingredients for meals which would ordinarily be taken on the wing: the coffee on the way to the Tube, the salad at lunch, the coming-home doughnut. There is a spike in sales of everything farming produces: beef, pork, potatoes. Everyone buys loads of milk and then realises they've got too much. Traditionally a nation which likes to spend as little on food as possible, the British change their habits overnight, spending an extra £1.4 billion in the four weeks to 22 April. Around three-quarters of households are buying red meat, a five-year high. Perhaps unsurprisingly, a month later a lot of us reported eating more than normal during lockdown.

The word 'unprecedented' gets used a lot, though for some there's a distinct sense of déjà vu. Farmers, uniquely sensitised to mass contagions, manage somehow to be among the most affected, and the least. Just as they did during foot-and-mouth, people remark on how strange it is listening to all this talk of death in the midst of the brightest spring in decades. It's lambing season, a time which always requires a kind of unrelenting introspection, though the difference this year is that most sheep farmers can't get any outside help from part-time workers or vet students so they're doing it all themselves. Lamb prices rise over Easter, then slump again, rise, drop. People take to home baking. Sales of butter and cream increase, no one can get flour for love nor money and people talk about sourdough cultures the way they used to talk about drug experiences. Calves are born, potatoes are planted, orchards blossom. Everyone worries that there won't be enough people to pick the crops. The livestock markets still operate, but behind closed doors. On auction days people drop their animals off at the entrance and are told later how much, or how little, they have sold for. Most people adapt, take things in their stride, get on. And, because no one can move, the oil price is low. Because the oil price is low, the cost of synthetic fabrics is low, and because the price is low, consumers (if they're buying at all) are buying those synthetics instead of wool. Suppliers are struggling to shift the stock they've got. All of which means that fleeces which might have sold for £1 a kilo a year ago are now selling for almost nothing.

Farmers have been rehearsing for this for a very long time – since farming began, almost. It is an industry inured to chronic volatility in a time of chronic volatility, to the gamble of ordinary life, to markets dropping or rising with neither notice nor explanation, to lifting every stone in search of other sources of income, to turning at speed. Big farms with complex supply chains stutter briefly, but continue. The demand for what they produce, and the will to get it onto the shelves, redoubles. Some small and medium-sized farms adapt quickly, making a virtue of being local, using social media. Others sell from the farm, or start delivering locally and then nationally. The market for organic food expands. Those who had been selling to restaurants start supplying shops or doing home deliveries instead. A few dairy farmers pick up local milk and egg rounds, others profit from the installation of sanitised vending machines from which they can sell everything they, and often their neighbours, produce. Helped by the dry weather, several enterprising fruit suppliers turn themselves into drive-through outlets for fresh fruit and veg. Because of the restrictions, a barter system develops: a supermarket run in return for hedge saplings, a few bales of hay in return for a couple of hours' chainsawing, an old cement mixer in return for a set of spare gates.

Many of those who struggle are those who, like the dairy sector, are on contract to sell a single product to one supplier or are heavily reliant on exports. Year on year, the UK dairy herd contracts by 2.9 per cent. Getting things in and out of the UK becomes more difficult: beef and lamb imports and exports both drop temporarily. The country in the city discovers the country outside the city. With all the advantages of urban life removed – culture, other people, internationalism – many people decide they'd rather not be there.

And like many other professions which prove useful in a pandemic – medicine, transport, electrics, tech – the social value of farming begins, very slowly, to shift. Partly it's the ancient pining for another life. But it's also the beginnings of a recognition that the green places produce something beyond just tourism revenue. Farmers, that tiny, endangered corner of the UK workforce, begin to appear less as obstacles to environmental progress than workers providing an essential we only just recognised. Food security, which hadn't even been a conversation before Covid-19, has reinstated itself on the agenda. Why, people wonder, if we have the material, physical, financial and technological capacity to grow so much of our own food in this country, do we not do so? The national conversation begins to slide from the things we want (services, clothes, holidays, property, shares, wealth) to the things we need (food, love, health, connection, home, outside).

At Rise the lawnmower is broken, so David moves the three tups into the cottage garden. Over the space of a fortnight or so the sheep strim through everything within a metre of soil level. The garden acquires a no-nonsense, no-vegetation appearance. The swallows return, adding their scribbles to the soft rip of new grass. Above them on the high field up the hill, the cows and their calves are thriving, sharing the grass with two hares and a few skylarks. Every morning a Land Rover and trailer rattle past, belonging to a farmer who has half his flock on grazing 12 miles away. The B&B in the farmhouse is paused, but other jobs take its place: the loan of kit to other farmers, repairing the quad, dealing with last winter's fallen trees, figuring out how exactly to plumb a new bathroom without the use of a plumber.

Bert's shape still outlines this farm but no longer with the same solidity. The division of the buildings has changed and renewed it, and the next generation is on its way. Brexit, Covid-19, lockdown and the recession have forced the pace, and things are changing. And maybe, just maybe, it's the world which turns this time. Small and medium-sized farms, caught in the backwash of obsolete policy, had begun to look antique, preservers of an outdated image. If we want to keep eating chicken at scale, then we have to farm them at scale. The same goes for all the things we want more of – fruit and veg, burgers, sausages, bread flour. But maybe, just maybe, Covid-19 has proved that the most sprightly small farms still have a role to play by being local, by adapting quickly and by being places which are trusted by the people who are near to them.

If you were to look at Rise it would seem almost exactly the same as ten years ago. The same buildings still wander along the side of the hill. Sheep still graze on the fields above and below. In the past few years a succession of swallows, house martins, wood pigeons, hares, badgers, owls, foxes, pheasants, rats, rabbits, magpies, mice, deer, blackbirds, bullfinches, ravens, sparrows, skylarks, sparrowhawks and buzzards have explored these grounds and found them good. Four sets of chickens have come, laid, and gone. Some of Rise's earth has washed down the hill to a bigger river far away, and other earth has arrived – on the wind, on the wheels of cars, washed in from above. Many of the farm's most prominent ash trees, big old beasts which have seen Rise through the twentieth century and beyond, are dying, their branches baring. Now the woodland has a patched, stark quality, as if two opposing seasons have arrived at once. Other things are flourishing: the calves, the grass, the sense of fresh intent. As Bryn shuffles sightlessly in the lane, tremulous on his last legs, the twins are born: two girls. The future.

Once every few years there's a heatwave and the outlines of the land come up altered, as if the colour of centuries had all drained off for a moment. Circles and squares rise up, lines resurge. Phantom mansions, long-gone airfields and spectral forts lift themselves from the parched barley, and with them comes the recognition that this land has been recycled a thousand times already, far before the Romans and long after all trace of us. Some sense of Bert's ability to see this place vertically has begun to trickle down. Not just through a better understanding of all the uses this land has been put to, but through all the lives which have long been spliced to it. This place is not just a farm or a view or a business, a classification or a record of all the attempts to pull money out of it. It's not even just a lineage of all the energy – human, animal, vegetative – changed in some way because of it. It's just itself. It just is.

And beyond this hill, out there in the rest of Britain, is another countryside. Along the roads, billboards announce MOTs, nursery places and NFU insurance, and every lay-by harbours a lost Hermes driver. There's a bus stop with a broken shelter and a column of black smoke suggestive of burned carpets. There are boarded-up pubs, forestry operations and archaeological sites, signs informing the passing motorist that LANE PRIORITIES HAVE CHANGED or CHRIST DIED. There are offers on windfall pears and Cockapoo pups, festoons of fresh electric fencing, discarded face masks and skeletal pylons. Empty industrial units square up the edges of the road and the council announces roadworks to be started last year. There are grit bins, dance classes, craft fairs and zip wires, CCTV in the trees and half a century of unmoved scrap. There are dead badgers ballooned by the side of the road and a bouquet of barred feathers risen up from the tarmac.

And away and beneath, in the places the roads will never reach, an older, deeper country lives on. Once in a while, walking home through the blue of an autumn dusk, time skids sideways. The line of the oak, the flare of the bonfire, the deep beat of approaching horses, belong to now and never and always, reminders of a wilder kind of land. There are still things hidden in the tangles of bracken and briar, kept safe in the hollows, waiting. And out beyond all of this is always a farm, and in every farm there is something going on which isn't at all like you think it is.

Useful terms

Arable land   Land used for growing crops.

BSE   Bovine Spongiform Encephalopathy (sometimes called 'mad cow disease'). A fatal neurodegenerative disease which can occur in cattle, and in rare cases has spread to humans.

Buck rake   A wide, toothed rake for gathering or turning hay.

Bullock   Castrated male calf.

Brash   Small branches and twigs from felled timber.

Byre   Cowshed.

Cast sheep   A sheep (often a heavily pregnant ewe) that has fallen onto its back and is unable to get back up again (also 'rigwelted').

Colostrum   The first milk produced by mammals (including ewes and cows) after giving birth.

Common land   Generally open upland areas on which there is a right to roam, and on which animals from different neighbouring farms are grazed.

Contract farming   Farm work carried out under the terms of a contract between the farmer/producer and the buyer/supplier. E.g. dairy farms under contract to produce milk for supermarkets.

Field Work

Cover crop	A crop planted to cover, protect and replenish the soil rather than as part of an annual harvest. E.g. turnips or brassicas in winter.
Cull ewes	Ewes that have reached the end of their productive lives.
Deadweight	Animal carcases sold according to the amount of saleable meat they will yield.
Drove roads	Tracks across country used for walking sheep and cattle to markets.
Ewe	Female sheep.
Fallen stock	Farm animals that have died naturally or after euthanasia, not destined for meat.
Fallow	Land that has been left uncultivated to allow it to rest from production.
Farm gate value	The cost of any item produced on a farm (e.g. milk) up to the point of sale from the farm but not including any subsequent processing and packaging.
Fodder	Any food, including hay, given to livestock.
Gilt	A sow who has yet to have her first litter.
Gimmer	A weaned ewe which has not yet been sheared, about six to fifteen months old.
Gleaning	Gathering unharvested crops from fields or farms.
Glebe	Cultivated land.
Harrow	An implement used to break up and smooth out ploughed soil in preparation for planting.
Hefted flock	A flock of sheep grazing within land they will not stray from.
Heifer	A cow over one year old which has not yet borne calves.

Useful terms

Hoggs Sheep of either sex between the weaning to first shearing age.

Husbandry The practice and skill of breeding and raising farmed animals.

In-bye Scottish/Northern term meaning the farmland closest to the farm buildings.

Lairage A temporary holding pen for animals.

Livestock Animals farmed for sale.

Liveweight The weight of a live animal.

Mastitis An infection of the udder, particularly in dairy cows.

Midden Rubbish heap.

Pannage Livestock, particularly pigs, released into woodland to forage.

Poached Damaged grassland caused by trampling, particularly after rain.

Quota Limitations imposed on the production of a commodity, e.g. milk.

Rise Yellowish line on sheep's fleece showing the point at which the new wool is beginning to lift away from the old. Evidence that the sheep are ready for shearing.

Ruminant Any animal (e.g. cattle) which chews the cud.

Set-aside Policy of taking land out of agricultural production.

Silage Grass cut and wilted but not completely dried (as it would be for hay), then wrapped in plastic or placed in a large mound or pit (called a clamp) from which air is excluded.

Standing straw Straw from (possibly damaged) crops sold unharvested.

Steer	Young castrated male cattle.
Stores	Cattle or sheep sold to 'finishers' before they're ready for slaughter and kept on a low-maintenance diet over winter.
Stubble	The part of a crop left in the ground after harvesting. E.g. oat or wheat stubble.
Suckler cow	The mother of a calf raised for beef production.
Topping off	Cutting back high growth on rough ground.
Tup	A male sheep, also called a ram.

Acknowledgements

A lot of people helped during the research for this book. Some explained, some allowed me to shadow them, and some also offered the chance of work. For every one person I've quoted directly, there are five or six others who provided vital background. I hope I've managed to repay all the generosity and trust which was shown to me by presenting a rounded picture of their worlds. If I have made factual mistakes, then I can only apologise and correct.

I've done my best to speak to farmers from all sectors and parts of the country. In the North, Bob, Jane, and Jon McCosh and Jenny Orr, John and Barbara Denning, and Michael and Tina Scott were all openhanded with their time and their hearts, and I hope I've done my best to respect that. In the South and West, thanks to Russ Carrington, Bill and Gail Quan and Anthony Roden, Nigel Winney and family, George and Anthony Snell, David Newport, Will Jackson and Ivor Snead, Ali Capper, Dave and Max Richards, Richard and Mary Bartle, Bruce and Lynn Davis, David and Gill Gwilt, and all the students who came to talk from Harper Adams (Matthew Rollaston, Rowan Boardley, Sophie Bell, Alice Clews, Jack Poulden, Emily Jones, Luke Ormond and Thomas Whittaker).

Down in Cornwall Claire Worden, NFYFC Vice Chair and campaigner on mental health issues, has been a clear-headed guide throughout. Clare Greener, the NFU's policy adviser in Herefordshire, was funny, patient and accommodating. Thanks too to Minette Batters, NFU President and Richard

Macdonald, Chair of the 2011 Farming Regulation Task Force for their time, and to both Claire Pillman and the pseudonymised civil servant for offering an impressively direct image of life on the far side of the paperwork.

Amongst the large-animal vets, I'm particularly grateful to Bill Main for allowing me to shadow him for several days with exceptional good grace, Peter Jinman for both information and editorial input, and to Navaratnam Partheeban, Nick Gibbon, Mike Bellamy, Dominic Alexander and Matthew Pugh for their insights into the tensions between farming's inner and outer worlds. In some places I have had to disguise names or details. Where I have, I am particularly grateful for the generosity and trust of those involved in giving me the chance to witness their work.

The two farming facilitators, Heather Wildman and Siân Bushell, offered a compelling portrait of the factors which make farming so unique, as did legal mediator Claire Jackson and Ifor Williams for the Farming Community Network. Lucy Reeves gave a sense of some of the obstacles to love in the countryside, and both the students at Fairfields School and Becky Tinson provided an endearingly heartfelt view of what it's like to grow up within farming.

And finally to all of those without whom this would never have got written at all: Colin and William Miles, John and Will Watkins, Ben Hillstead, Rob Curtis, Debs and Dilwyn Davies, Kenton Lloyd, and Pete and Cam Archer. All of them put up with a lot of questions, mostly about sheep. Most of all to Russell and Lesley Whistance, and to Pat. Some of the finer details may be awry, but I hope I've got the gist. To Cecily Gayford for outstanding displays of patience, and to Victoria Hobbs, friend and special agent.